DANUBE CRUISE TRAVEL GUIDE

2024 Edition

Cruising the Danube: Unlock the Wonders of Central Europe, Plan Your Ideal Cruise Itinerary, and Make the Most of Your Danube Adventure

By

Roy McKean

TABLE OF CONTENT

CHAPTER THREE

DESTINATIONS ALONG THE DANUBE

CHAPTER FOUR

ONBOARD EXPERIENCE

CHAPTER FIVE

EXPLORING CULTURE AND HISTORY

5.1 UNESCO WORLD HERITAGE SITES ALONG THE DANUBE

5.1.1 Vienna: Historic Centre of the Austrian Capital

5.1.2 Budapest: Banks of the Danube, Buda Castle Quarter, and Andrássy Avenue

5.1.3 WACHAU CULTURAL LANDSCAPE

5.1.4 Český Krumlov: Historic Centre and Castle

5.1.5 Regensburg: Old Town with Stadtamhof

5.1.6 The Danube Delta

5.2. MUSEUMS, GALLERIES, AND HISTORICAL LANDMARKS

CHAPTER SIX

PRACTICAL TIPS FOR A SMOOTH CRUISE

6.1. PACKING ESSENTIALS FOR YOUR DANUBE RIVER ADVENTURE

6.2. HEALTH AND SAFETY CONSIDERATIONS

6.3. CURRENCY AND PAYMENT TIPS

6.4. COMMUNICATION AND CONNECTIVITY

CHAPTER SEVEN

BEYOND THE CRUISE: EXTENDING YOUR DANUBE EXPERIENCE

7.1 PRE- AND POST-CRUISE EXTENSIONS

7.1.1: Pre-Cruise Exploration

7.1.2: Post-Cruise Unwind

7.1.3: Crafting Your Own Extension

7.2 ALTERNATIVE TRAVEL OPTIONS ALONG THE DANUBE

7.3 SUSTAINABLE TRAVEL PRACTICES

CONCLUSION

Reflecting on Your Danube River Cruise Experience

Continued Exploration: Other River Cruises and Travel Adventures

DISCLAIMER

Welcome to our immersive travel guide! As you embark on this journey through the pages of Danube River Cruise travel guide, we want to set clear expectations. While we aim to transport you to captivating destinations and provide valuable insights, we do so without the aid of maps and images.

Why, you ask?

Our intention is simple: to stimulate your imagination and curiosity. By omitting maps, we encourage you to rely on your instincts, engage with locals, and discover hidden gems beyond the well-trodden paths. Instead of images, we invite you to paint vivid mental pictures through words and descriptions, allowing your mind to craft its unique interpretation of the places we explore.

In this text-centric guide, we prioritize storytelling, history, culture, and practical advice. We believe that your own perceptions and interpretations will make your travels more personal and memorable. It's an invitation to be present in the moment, to interact with your surroundings, and to embrace the serendipitous adventures that come your way.

So, as you delve into these pages, let your imagination soar, and let the words be your compass in this world of exploration and discovery.

INTRODUCTION

Welcome to the Danube: The Blue Ribbon of Europe

The Danube River, often referred to as the "Blue Ribbon of Europe," weaves its way through the heart of the continent, connecting diverse cultures, histories, and landscapes. This iconic river, the second-longest in Europe, holds a special place in the hearts of travelers seeking a unique and enriching experience. As you embark on your journey along the Danube, you'll be captivated by the river's beauty, charm, and the rich tapestry of stories that unfold along its shores.

The Danube River stretches across ten countries, making it a true international waterway that has witnessed centuries of human history. From its source in the Black Forest of Germany to its delta in the Black Sea, the Danube traverses a remarkable 2,857 kilometers (1,775 miles). Its significance goes beyond being a mere geographical feature; it has been a lifeline for countless civilizations, a trade route for merchants, and a source of inspiration for artists and poets.

One cannot truly appreciate the Danube without understanding its historical and cultural significance. The river has been a witness to the rise and fall of empires, the birth of nations, and the ebb and flow of trade and commerce. As you navigate its waters, you'll encounter remnants of ancient civilizations, medieval castles perched on hillsides, and vibrant cities that have evolved with the passage of time.

The term "Blue Ribbon of Europe" aptly describes the Danube's striking blue color, which has inspired poets and musicians alike. This distinctive hue is attributed to the high sediment load carried by the river, creating a mesmerizing spectacle as it winds its way through valleys and plains. The beauty of the Danube is not confined to its waters alone; it extends to the picturesque landscapes that unfold along its banks, featuring vineyards, forests, and charming villages that seem frozen in time.

Embarking on a journey along the Danube is not just a cruise; it's an exploration of Europe's cultural mosaic. The river serves as a connecting thread between nations, fostering a sense of unity and diversity. From the grandeur of Vienna's imperial palaces to the lively spirit of Budapest's vibrant markets, each stop along the Danube offers a unique glimpse into the region's past and present.

For those considering a Danube River cruise, the experience goes beyond the allure of luxurious ships and impeccable service. It's about immersing oneself in the stories etched into the riverbanks, engaging with local communities, and savoring the flavors of regional cuisines. The Danube invites travelers to slow down, to appreciate the unfolding landscapes, and to connect with the people who call its shores home.

Whether you are a history enthusiast, a lover of art and architecture, or simply someone seeking a tranquil escape, the Danube has something to offer. The river's cultural significance is complemented by the warm hospitality of the communities that have thrived along its course for centuries.

Each bend in the river brings forth new discoveries, inviting you to embrace the magic of the Blue Ribbon of Europe.

Why Choose a Danube River Cruise?

The allure of a Danube River cruise lies in its unique blend of history, culture, and breathtaking landscapes. As one of Europe's major rivers, the Danube meanders through ten countries, offering a diverse and captivating journey for travelers seeking an unforgettable experience. There are several compelling reasons why choosing a Danube River cruise is an exceptional travel option.

1. Rich Cultural Tapestry:

Embarking on a Danube River cruise means immersing yourself in the heart of Europe's rich cultural tapestry. The river flows through iconic cities like Vienna, Budapest, and Bratislava, each boasting its own unique history and charm. From grand palaces to medieval castles, the Danube is a gateway to centuries of European heritage. Travelers can explore museums, art galleries, and architectural wonders, gaining insight into the region's diverse cultural influences.

2. Scenic Landscapes and Charming Villages:

The Danube River journey is not just about cities; it's about the picturesque landscapes and charming villages that line its banks. As the cruise sails through the Wachau Valley, passengers are treated to vineyards, rolling hills, and storybook villages. The scenic beauty of the Danube Valley, a UNESCO World Heritage site, provides a serene backdrop for the entire voyage. It's a visual feast for nature enthusiasts and those seeking a peaceful escape.

3. Hassle-Free Travel Experience:

Opting for a Danube River cruise offers a hassle-free travel experience. Unlike traditional land-based tours, a river cruise allows you to unpack once and enjoy the journey without the stress of constant packing and unpacking. The cruise ship becomes a floating hotel, transporting you seamlessly from one enchanting destination to another. This convenience enhances the overall travel experience, providing more time to savor the sights and experiences along the Danube.

4. Unique Access to Historical Landmarks:

The Danube River is a gateway to historical landmarks that may be inaccessible by other means of transportation. Cruising along the river grants travelers unique access to significant sites, including ancient fortresses, medieval towns, and centuries-old castles. Some of these landmarks hold tales of battles, royal intrigues, and the evolution of European civilization, making the cruise a living history lesson.

5. Culinary Delights:

One of the highlights of a Danube River cruise is the opportunity to savor the diverse culinary offerings of the region. Each city along the route boasts its own gastronomic delights, and onboard the cruise ship, passengers can enjoy a curated selection of local and international cuisines. From traditional Austrian schnitzel to Hungarian goulash, the culinary journey along the Danube is a feast for the taste buds.

6. Intimate and Personalized Experience:

Compared to larger ocean cruises, a Danube River cruise offers a more intimate and personalized experience. With a smaller passenger capacity, cruise-goers can enjoy a relaxed atmosphere, personalized service, and the chance to connect with fellow travelers. The smaller size of the ship also allows for docking in the heart of city centers, providing easy access to attractions and cultural hotspots.

7. Unwind in Luxury:

Danube River cruises often feature luxurious amenities, from well-appointed cabins to gourmet dining options and wellness facilities. Travelers can unwind in style, enjoying the comfort and elegance of the cruise ship while taking in the ever-changing scenery along the riverbanks. It's a perfect blend of indulgence and adventure, creating a truly memorable travel experience.

What to Expect from This Guide

1. Unlocking the Danube's Secrets:

Embark on a seamless exploration of the Danube, a river that has played a pivotal role in shaping the history and culture of the regions it traverses. This guide is not merely a collection of facts but a narrative that unravels the secrets and stories hidden within the winding waters of the Danube. From its origin in the Black Forest to its majestic flow through ten countries, each chapter reveals a new layer of the Danube's charm.

2. Comprehensive Planning for Your Voyage:

One of the key features of this guide is its dedicated section on planning. Whether you are a first-time cruiser or a seasoned traveler, our comprehensive insights into choosing the perfect cruise itinerary, understanding the best times to embark on your journey, and practical budgeting tips ensure that your planning process is stress-free and tailored to your preferences.

3. Onboard Experience Unveiled:

What sets this guide apart is its in-depth exploration of the onboard experience. Step aboard your cruise ship with confidence, armed with knowledge about the amenities, services, and safety guidelines. From the moment you set foot on the deck, you'll find yourself immersed in a world of luxury, comfort, and entertainment. Navigate the rules and etiquettes to make the most of your time on the water.

4. City Highlights and Hidden Gems:

Prepare to be captivated by the charm of cities lining the Danube. Our guide meticulously covers key destinations such as Vienna, Budapest, and Bratislava, offering a curated selection of must-visit landmarks and hidden gems. Dive into the cultural tapestry of each city, exploring historical sites, indulging in local cuisine, and connecting with the vibrant local communities.

5. Cultural Immersion and Enrichment:

This guide goes beyond the surface, providing a deep dive into cultural immersion along the Danube. Delve into the arts and architecture that line the riverbanks, savor the gastronomic treasures unique to each region, and discover the joy of connecting with locals through enriching cultural experiences. This chapter is designed to enhance your understanding of the diverse cultures that thrive along the Danube.

6. Activities and Excursions for Every Taste:

Whether you seek historical landmarks, outdoor adventures, or onboard relaxation, this guide has you covered. Explore comprehensive sections on shore excursions, outdoor activities, and onboard entertainment. Tailor your experience to your preferences, ensuring that every moment along the Danube is crafted to suit your interests.

7. Practical Tips for a Seamless Journey:

Packing can be a daunting task, but fear not – our guide provides a detailed checklist of essentials for your river cruise. Additionally, discover photography tips to capture the Danube's beauty in all its glory. The guide also offers insights into making the most of your cruise experience, ensuring that you leave with cherished memories and a longing to return.

CHAPTER ONE

THE DANUBE IN PERSPECTIVE

1.1 The Danube's Historical Significance

The Danube River, often referred to as "Europe's Amazon," is more than just a majestic waterway winding through the heart of the continent. Its historical significance is deeply intertwined with the cultural tapestry of the regions it touches, making it a living testament to the ebb and flow of European history.

The roots of the Danube's historical importance can be traced back to ancient times. In the Roman era, the river served as a natural frontier, marking the northern boundary of the Roman Empire. The Romans referred to it as the "Danuvius," and it played a crucial role in shaping the geopolitics of the time. This mighty river not only delineated borders but also facilitated trade and communication between the Roman provinces.

As the centuries unfolded, the Danube continued to play a pivotal role in the rise and fall of empires. During the Middle Ages, it became a vital trade route for the burgeoning city-states and kingdoms along its banks. The Hanseatic League, a medieval trading alliance, recognized the economic potential of the Danube and sought to harness its navigational advantages.

The Ottoman Empire, at the height of its power, extended its influence along the Danube's lower reaches. The river became a strategic frontier between the Ottoman Empire and the Habsburg Monarchy, leading to centuries of conflicts and battles for control over its valuable waters.

The Danube's historical significance is also deeply embedded in the stories of the diverse cultures that flourished along its shores. From the elegant cities of Vienna and Budapest to the picturesque towns of Germany and the Balkans, the river has been witness to the rise of great civilizations. Castles, fortresses, and medieval towns that dot the riverbanks stand as silent sentinels to the tales of conquests, alliances, and cultural exchanges that unfolded along the Danube's course.

In the 19th and 20th centuries, the Danube played a central role in the industrialization and economic development of the regions it traversed. The river became a conduit for transporting goods, connecting inland cities to the Black Sea and beyond. Industrial hubs emerged along its banks, transforming the landscape and contributing to the growth of European economies.

However, the 20th century also brought challenges to the Danube's historical narrative. The river, once a symbol of unity, became a geopolitical frontier during the Cold War, dividing Eastern and Western Europe. The Iron Curtain cast its shadow over the Danube, restricting navigation and stifling the natural flow of cultural exchange.

With the fall of the Iron Curtain and the reunification of Europe, the Danube regained its role as a unifying force. The European Union's expansion eastward brought new opportunities for cooperation and shared prosperity along the river. Today, the Danube stands as a symbol of European unity and a testament to the resilience of nations overcoming historical divides.

1.2. Geographical Overview of the Danube River

Spanning over 1,700 miles (2,850 kilometers), the Danube is the second-longest river in Europe after the Volga. Its course takes it through ten countries, making it a vital lifeline and a symbol of unity in a region known for its rich history and diverse landscapes.

Geographical Origins:

The Danube River has its humble beginnings in the Black Forest region of Germany, where the two small tributaries, the Brigach and Breg rivers, converge near the town of Donaueschingen. From this confluence, the river embarks on its long journey southeastward, passing through a multitude of landscapes, climates, and cultures.

Flowing through Multiple Countries:

The Danube River flows through or forms the borders of ten countries, showcasing the immense geographical diversity of Central and Southeastern Europe. These countries include Germany, Austria, Slovakia, Hungary, Croatia, Serbia, Bulgaria, Romania, Moldova, and Ukraine. Each country along the Danube has its own unique influence on the river's character, contributing to the richness of the surrounding landscapes and cultural heritage.

Connecting Capitals and Cities:

The Danube River has played a crucial role in shaping the development of major European cities. As it meanders through the continent, it passes by or near iconic capitals such as Vienna (Austria), Budapest (Hungary), and Belgrade (Serbia). The river serves as a natural highway, connecting these urban centers and facilitating trade, transportation, and cultural exchange.

Diverse Landscapes Along the Danube:

The geographical features along the Danube are as varied as the countries it traverses. In the upper course, the river flows through the picturesque landscapes of the Bavarian and Austrian Alps, characterized by lush forests, charming villages, and alpine meadows. As it progresses southeastward, the Danube transitions into the expansive Pannonian Plain, with vast agricultural fields and historic towns dotting the landscape.

Navigating the Danube Gorge:

One of the most visually striking sections of the Danube is the Iron Gate, a narrow gorge that forms a natural border between Serbia and Romania. Here, the river cuts through the Southern Carpathian Mountains, creating a dramatic and scenic landscape. The Iron Gate not only presents a visual spectacle but also challenges river navigation, showcasing the dynamic nature of the Danube's course.

Ecological Importance:

Beyond its cultural and historical significance, the Danube River is an essential ecological corridor, supporting a diverse range of flora and fauna. The river and its surrounding wetlands provide habitats for numerous species, including fish, birds, and mammals. Efforts have been made to preserve the ecological integrity of the Danube, with initiatives aimed at sustainable management and conservation.

Human Interaction and Utilization:

Throughout history, the Danube has been a vital resource for the people living along its banks. Its waters have powered mills, supported agriculture, and facilitated trade and transportation. In the modern era, the river continues to serve as a crucial waterway for shipping, with the construction of locks and dams to regulate water levels and facilitate navigation.

Challenges and Environmental Concerns:

Despite its significance, the Danube faces various environmental challenges. Pollution, habitat degradation, and changes in water flow due to human activities pose threats to the river's ecosystem. Efforts by the countries along the Danube, as well as collaborative initiatives, aim to address these challenges and ensure the long-term sustainability of this vital watercourse.

Cultural Heritage Along the Danube:

The Danube River is a living testament to the cultural diversity of Europe. Its banks are adorned with historic castles, fortresses, and charming villages, each bearing the imprint of the civilizations that have flourished along its shores. The river has been a witness to the rise and fall of empires, the exchange of ideas, and the blending of traditions.

1.3. Understanding the Danube's Cultural Impact
Historical Significance:

The Danube River has witnessed the rise and fall of empires, the clash of civilizations, and the ebb and flow of historical events. From the Roman Empire to the Austro-Hungarian Empire, the Danube has been a strategic lifeline, facilitating trade, migration, and cultural exchange. The riverbanks are adorned with remnants of ancient civilizations, including Roman fortifications, medieval castles, and charming old towns that bear witness to the region's turbulent past. Navigating the Danube is like embarking on a journey through time, with each bend in the river revealing layers of history and cultural evolution.

Cultural Diversity Along the Danube:

The Danube is a melting pot of cultures, with its course passing through or alongside ten different countries, including Germany, Austria, Slovakia, Hungary, Croatia, Serbia, Bulgaria, Romania, Moldova, and Ukraine. Each of these nations contributes its own unique traditions, customs, and heritage to the tapestry of Danube culture. From the classical elegance of Vienna to the vibrant folklore of Budapest and the Slavic influences in Belgrade, the Danube reflects a kaleidoscope of cultural diversity that is truly unparalleled.

Architectural Marvels:

The cities along the Danube boast architectural wonders that bear testament to the various periods of history they have endured. Vienna, for example, showcases imperial palaces and grand Baroque structures, while Budapest boasts a stunning panorama of Gothic, Renaissance, and Ottoman architecture. The blend of architectural styles along the Danube is a visual representation of the confluence of different cultural influences over the centuries. Exploring the cathedrals, palaces, and town squares along the river provides a tangible link to the past and an appreciation for the enduring impact of diverse cultural elements.

Art and Literature Inspired by the Danube:

The Danube has long been a muse for artists and writers, inspiring countless works of art and literature. The river's serene beauty, picturesque landscapes, and the romantic allure of its cities have been captured in paintings, poems, and novels throughout the ages. The works of artists like Albrecht Dürer, who found inspiration in the Danube's landscapes, and writers like Claudio Magris, who penned the acclaimed "Danube" exploring the river's cultural and historical significance, stand as tributes to the profound impact of the river on the creative spirit.

Culinary Traditions and Gastronomic Delights:

One cannot truly understand the cultural impact of the Danube without savoring the culinary delights that define the regions along its banks. Each city boasts its own gastronomic traditions, blending local ingredients and culinary techniques. From the hearty goulash of Hungary to the delicate pastries of Austria, the Danube is a gastronomic journey that mirrors the diversity of the cultures it connects. Exploring local markets, tasting traditional dishes, and indulging in regional specialties is an integral part of experiencing the Danube's cultural richness.

Festivals and Celebrations:

The Danube comes alive with festivals and celebrations that reflect the cultural vibrancy of the communities along its shores. Whether it's the lively Danube Carnival in Germany, the Budapest Wine Festival, or the Belgrade Boat Carnival, these events showcase the traditions, music, and dance that have been passed down through generations. Participating in these festivities provides travelers with a firsthand experience of the dynamic and celebratory spirit that defines Danube culture.

Local Customs and Traditions:

Understanding the cultural impact of the Danube involves immersing oneself in the daily lives of the people who call its banks home. From the laid-back coffee culture of Vienna to the thermal baths of Budapest and the folklore festivals in rural Romania, each stretch of the river introduces visitors to distinct local customs and traditions. Engaging with the communities along the Danube allows for a deeper appreciation of the ways in which cultural heritage is preserved and celebrated.

CHAPTER TWO

PLANNING YOUR DANUBE RIVER CRUISE

2.1 Selecting the Right Cruise Line for You

Embarking on a Danube River cruise is an exciting prospect, and one of the crucial decisions you'll make is choosing the right cruise line. The plethora of options available can be overwhelming, but by considering various factors, you can ensure that your cruise aligns perfectly with your preferences and expectations.

1. Cruise Line Reputation:

When evaluating cruise lines, reputation speaks volumes. Conduct thorough research by reading reviews from fellow travelers, consulting travel forums, and exploring social media groups dedicated to cruise enthusiasts. A reputable cruise line with positive customer feedback is likely to provide a more enjoyable experience.

2. Itinerary and Destinations:

Each cruise line may offer a slightly different itinerary, with variations in the cities visited and the duration of shore excursions. Consider what destinations you find most appealing and ensure the cruise line you choose covers those locations. Whether you're drawn to the historic charm of Vienna, the vibrant energy of Budapest, or the cultural richness of Bratislava, make sure the itinerary aligns with your interests.

3. Onboard Amenities and Services:

Cruise ships vary widely in terms of onboard amenities and services. Some cater to a more luxurious experience with gourmet dining, spa facilities, and entertainment options, while others focus on a more casual and relaxed atmosphere. Evaluate what is essential to you – whether it's fine dining, fitness facilities, or entertainment – and choose a cruise line that aligns with your preferences.

4. Cabin Options:

The type of cabin you choose can significantly impact your cruise experience. Cruise lines offer various cabin categories, from standard cabins to luxurious suites. Consider your budget, desired level of comfort, and any specific requirements you may have. If you plan to spend a significant amount of time in your cabin, opting for a more spacious and well-appointed accommodation might be worth the investment.

5. Entertainment and Activities:

Cruises are not just about the destinations; they also offer a range of onboard activities and entertainment. Some cruise lines focus on cultural enrichment, offering lectures and workshops, while others prioritize lively entertainment, including live performances and themed parties. Assess the cruise line's approach to onboard activities to ensure it aligns with your interests and expectations.

6. Cruise Atmosphere:

Cruise lines often have distinct atmospheres catering to different demographics. Some may appeal to families with a more casual and family-friendly vibe, while others cater to adults seeking a quieter and more sophisticated experience. Consider the atmosphere you desire and choose a cruise line that aligns with your preferences to ensure a comfortable and enjoyable journey.

7. Inclusive Packages and Additional Costs:

Carefully review the cruise line's pricing structure to understand what is included in the initial cost and what may incur additional charges. Some cruise lines offer all-inclusive packages that cover meals, beverages, and excursions, while others may require separate payments for certain amenities. Being aware of potential additional costs can help you budget more effectively.

8. Special Offers and Discounts:

Keep an eye out for special offers, discounts, and promotions provided by cruise lines. Many offer early booking incentives, loyalty programs, or seasonal discounts. Taking advantage of these opportunities can not only save you money but also enhance your overall cruise experience.

2.2 Choosing the Best Time to Cruise the Danube

Selecting the optimal time for a Danube River cruise is a crucial aspect of planning a memorable and enjoyable journey. The timing of your cruise can significantly impact your overall experience, influencing everything from weather conditions to the cultural events you might encounter along the way. In this section, we'll delve into the various seasons and considerations to help you choose the best time to embark on your Danube adventure.

Spring Splendor: March to May

Spring is a captivating time to cruise the Danube, as nature awakens from its winter slumber, and vibrant hues blanket the riverbanks. March marks the beginning of the cruising season, with milder temperatures and blooming landscapes. As you sail through cities like Vienna and Budapest, you'll witness cherry blossoms and tulips in full bloom, creating a picturesque backdrop for your journey. The pleasant weather during spring allows for comfortable exploration of onshore attractions, and the tourist crowds are generally more manageable than during peak summer months.

However, it's essential to note that early spring can still bring cooler temperatures, and occasional rain showers are not uncommon. Therefore, packing layers and rain-resistant gear is advisable to ensure you're prepared for any weather surprises.

Summer Sunshine: June to August

Summer is the high season for Danube River cruises, and for good reason. The weather is at its warmest, with long, sunny days creating an ideal setting for exploring both on and off the ship. The summer months offer a diverse range of activities, from leisurely strolls through historic cities to outdoor excursions along the riverbanks.

Cruising during the summer allows you to fully appreciate the beauty of the Danube's landscapes. The lush greenery, clear skies, and vibrant atmosphere make for an enchanting experience. Keep in mind that with the favorable weather comes increased tourist traffic. Popular attractions may be busier, and it's advisable to plan and book excursions in advance to secure your spot.

Autumn Elegance: September to November

Fall brings a different kind of charm to the Danube region, with changing foliage painting the landscape in warm hues of red, orange, and gold. September and October are particularly delightful months for a cruise, offering pleasant temperatures and a more relaxed atmosphere compared to the bustling summer season.

Autumn cruises provide a unique perspective as you meander through picturesque vineyards and witness the harvest season. The crisp air and fewer crowds allow for a more intimate exploration of cities like Regensburg and Linz. Additionally, many cultural events and festivals take place during the fall, providing an opportunity to immerse yourself in local traditions and celebrations.

Winter Whimsy: December to February

While winter may not be the most popular time for a Danube River cruise, it has its own magical allure, especially for those who appreciate a quieter and more intimate atmosphere. Cruises during December offer a festive experience with Christmas markets adorning the riverbanks in cities like Nuremberg and Vienna.

Sailing during the winter months provides a unique perspective on the Danube's beauty, with a chance to see historic sites dusted with snow. Some cruise lines offer special holiday-themed itineraries, allowing you to embrace the enchantment of a European winter wonderland.

However, it's essential to be prepared for colder temperatures during winter cruises. Layered clothing, thermal wear, and winter accessories will ensure your comfort as you explore the charming cities along the Danube.

Considerations for Your Cruise Timing

Beyond the seasons, several factors should influence your decision on when to embark on a Danube River cruise:

- Cultural and Festive Events: Research and consider if there are any specific cultural events, festivals, or celebrations happening along the Danube during your preferred time of travel. Participating in local festivities can enhance your overall experience.
- River Levels: Keep in mind that river levels can fluctuate, affecting the navigability of certain stretches. While cruise lines are adept at managing these variations, it's always good to be aware of potential impacts on your itinerary.
- Personal Preferences: Consider your own preferences when it comes to weather, crowd sizes, and the type of experience you desire. Whether you enjoy the vibrancy of summer or the tranquility of winter, aligning your cruise with your preferences ensures a more fulfilling journey.

2.3 Itinerary Options: From Vienna to Budapest and Beyond

Exploring the Danube River on a cruise unveils a tapestry of enchanting cities, each with its unique charm and historical significance. Among the numerous itinerary options, the journey from Vienna to Budapest stands out as a classic and captivating route. This route not only traverses two of Europe's most iconic cities but also unveils the cultural richness and natural beauty that line the Danube.

Vienna: The Imperial City

Commencing your Danube River cruise in Vienna is an exquisite choice. The Austrian capital, known as the "City of Music," is steeped in imperial history and architectural splendor. As the cruise sets sail from Vienna, passengers are treated to breathtaking views of the city's iconic landmarks, including the stately Schoenbrunn Palace and the historic Belvedere.

The city's cultural richness is a theme that persists throughout the voyage. Travelers can immerse themselves in the melodies of classical music with a visit to the grand Vienna State Opera or explore the intricate exhibits at the Kunsthistorisches Museum. The culinary scene in Vienna is equally enticing, with coffeehouses offering a delightful array of pastries and traditional Viennese dishes.

Bratislava: Where History Meets Modernity

As the Danube flows eastward, the cruise docks at Bratislava, the charming capital of Slovakia. Nestled along the riverbanks, Bratislava seamlessly combines its rich history with a modern and vibrant atmosphere. The iconic Bratislava Castle stands proudly on a hill overlooking the city, providing a picturesque backdrop for exploration.

Wandering through the cobbled streets of the Old Town, visitors encounter medieval charm alongside contemporary art installations. The unique blend of old and new is particularly evident in Bratislava's culinary offerings, where traditional Slovak dishes are served in trendy eateries.

Dürnstein: A Fairytale Stop

As the Danube winds through the Wachau Valley, a stop in Dürnstein feels like stepping into a fairytale. This small Austrian town is renowned for its medieval castle ruins perched high above the Danube and the vibrant blue and white baroque-style Stift Dürnstein abbey.

Exploring Dürnstein by foot allows travelers to soak in the idyllic scenery of vineyards and apricot orchards. Tasting the local wines, especially the famous Grüner Veltliner, adds a delightful touch to the cultural experience. The intimate size of Dürnstein provides a contrast to the larger cities along the route, allowing for a more leisurely and immersive exploration.

Budapest: A Tale of Two Cities

The climax of the journey is the majestic city of Budapest, often referred to as the "Paris of the East." Budapest, Hungary's capital, is a fusion of Buda and Pest, two distinct parts of the city separated by the Danube River. Each side has its own character, offering a diverse range of experiences for cruise travelers.

Buda, with its historic Castle Hill and Fisherman's Bastion, exudes a medieval charm, while Pest is a bustling hub of contemporary culture, shopping, and nightlife. The iconic Chain Bridge connects the two sides, creating a visual spectacle during the evening when Budapest is illuminated.

Beyond the Classics: Extended Danube Exploration

While the Vienna to Budapest route is a quintessential Danube River cruise experience, those seeking a more extensive adventure can opt for extended itineraries that go beyond these two cities. Extended cruises may continue eastward to explore lesser-known gems such as the medieval town of Pécs in Hungary or the Serbian capital, Belgrade.

Continuing the journey downstream opens up opportunities to delve into the cultural diversity of Eastern Europe. Cities like Novi Sad, with its vibrant arts scene, and the Romanian gem, Timisoara, known as the birthplace of the 1989 revolution, offer a deeper understanding of the region's complex history and contemporary vitality.

Customizing Your Danube Experience

Cruise operators often provide the flexibility for passengers to customize their itineraries, allowing for a tailored experience based on personal preferences. Whether it's an interest in wine tasting, historical exploration, or simply enjoying the scenic beauty of the Danube, travelers can choose excursions and activities that align with their passions.

2.4. Tips for Booking and Preparing for Your Journey

Embarking on a Danube River cruise is an exciting adventure, and proper planning is essential to ensure a smooth and enjoyable journey. In this section, we'll delve into valuable tips for booking your cruise and preparing for the unforgettable experience that awaits you along the majestic Danube.

1. Research Cruise Options

Before booking your Danube River cruise, take the time to research different cruise options available. Each cruise line may offer unique itineraries, onboard amenities, and excursion packages. Consider your preferences, such as the duration of the cruise, the destinations you wish to visit, and the type of onboard experience you desire. Whether you're looking for a cultural immersion, scenic landscapes, or a culinary journey, there's a cruise tailored to meet your interests.

2. Choose the Right Time to Cruise

The timing of your Danube River cruise can significantly impact your experience. Research the best time to visit based on your preferences and interests. The spring and fall seasons are popular for mild weather and fewer crowds, offering a more relaxed and immersive experience. Summer brings warmer temperatures but may also attract more tourists. Winter cruises provide a unique charm with festive holiday markets along the Danube, perfect for those seeking a magical winter getaway.

3. Budget Considerations

Setting a budget for your Danube River cruise is crucial in ensuring a stress-free journey. Take into account the cost of the cruise itself, as well as additional expenses such as excursions, gratuities, and onboard activities. Some cruise lines may include certain amenities in their upfront costs, while others may offer more à la carte options. Factor in pre-cruise expenses like flights and pre-cruise accommodation to create a comprehensive budget that aligns with your financial plan.

4. Booking in Advance

Once you've chosen your ideal cruise, consider booking well in advance to secure the best cabin options and take advantage of early booking discounts. Danube River cruises are popular, especially during peak seasons, and booking early ensures availability and the best rates. Keep an eye out for promotions and special offers, as cruise lines often provide deals for early bookings or last-minute reservations.

5. Understanding Cabin Categories

Danube River cruise ships offer a variety of cabin categories, each with its own set of amenities and views. Understand the differences between standard cabins, suites, and balcony cabins to make an informed decision based on your preferences and budget. While a balcony cabin provides stunning views from the privacy of your room, standard cabins may offer a more economical choice for those who plan to spend more time exploring onshore.

6. Pack Strategically

Packing efficiently is key to a comfortable and enjoyable cruise experience. Check the weather forecast for the duration of your cruise and pack accordingly. Comfortable walking shoes, layered clothing, and a versatile jacket are essentials for exploring onshore. Many cruises have casual dress codes, but you may also want to pack some formal wear for special events or dining experiences. Don't forget essentials such as travel adapters, toiletries, and any necessary medications.

7. Travel Insurance

Consider purchasing travel insurance to safeguard your investment in case of unforeseen circumstances. Travel insurance can cover trip cancellations, medical emergencies, and lost or delayed baggage. While it may seem like an additional expense, the peace of mind it provides is invaluable, especially when traveling to different countries with varying healthcare systems and unexpected travel disruptions.

8. Document Requirements

Ensure that you have all the necessary travel documents before setting sail on your Danube River cruise. Check passport expiration dates, visa requirements for the countries you'll be visiting, and any other documentation needed for your journey. Some cruise lines may assist with visa arrangements, but it's essential to verify and complete any required paperwork well in advance.

9. Stay Informed About Cruise Policies

Stay informed about the cruise line's policies, including cancellation policies, onboard protocols, and any health and safety measures in place. Familiarize yourself with the terms and conditions of your booking to avoid any surprises. Understanding the cruise line's policies ensures a smoother experience and allows you to make informed decisions throughout your journey.

10. Connect with Fellow Travelers

Joining online forums or social media groups related to Danube River cruises can be a valuable resource for tips, recommendations, and connecting with fellow travelers. Engaging with others who have embarked on similar journeys can provide insights into the cruise experience, onshore excursions, and hidden gems along the Danube.

By following these tips for booking and preparing for your Danube River cruise, you'll set the stage for a memorable and enriching journey. From selecting the right cruise to packing thoughtfully and staying informed, careful planning ensures that you can fully immerse yourself in the beauty and culture of this iconic European waterway.

2.5. Boarding the Cruise Ship: What to Expect

Embarking on a Danube River cruise is an exciting adventure, and as you approach the moment of boarding the cruise ship, there are several aspects to anticipate. This chapter provides an in-depth look at the experience of boarding a Danube River cruise ship, offering insights into what passengers can expect and how to make the most of this initial phase of their journey.

1. Arrival at the Port: Anticipation and Preparation

As you arrive at the port where your Danube River cruise ship is docked, the sense of anticipation is palpable. Ports along the Danube, such as those in Vienna, Budapest, and Bratislava, are often bustling hubs with a vibrant atmosphere. It's essential to arrive with ample time before the scheduled departure to ensure a smooth boarding process.

Upon arrival, port staff will guide you through the initial check-in procedures. Be prepared to present your identification, travel documents, and cruise reservation details. Most cruise lines also provide luggage tags for easy identification and delivery of your belongings to your cabin. It's advisable to keep essential items such as medications, important documents, and valuables in your carry-on bag.

2. Security and Screening: Ensuring Passenger Safety

Just like at airports, cruise terminals implement security measures to ensure the safety of all passengers. Expect to pass through security screening, where your bags will be scanned, and you may be required to walk through a metal detector. These measures are in place to guarantee a secure environment for everyone on board. Familiarize yourself with any specific guidelines provided by the cruise line to expedite this process.

3. Check-In and Documentation: Smooth Transition to Onboard Bliss

After passing through security, you'll proceed to the cruise check-in counter. Cruise staff will verify your identity, collect necessary documentation, and provide you with your cabin key or key card. This card serves as your identification, onboard charge card, and access key to your cabin. Take a moment to review the ship's layout map provided at check-in, helping you navigate the vessel with ease.

During the check-in process, you may also have the opportunity to book dining reservations, spa treatments, and shore excursions. If you haven't pre-booked these activities, it's a convenient time to plan and secure your preferred times and experiences.

4. Welcoming Aboard: First Impressions of the Ship

Stepping onto the cruise ship is a moment of awe and excitement. The welcoming atmosphere is enhanced by the friendly and attentive crew members ready to assist you. Take a moment to absorb the elegant decor and ambiance of the ship's common areas. Most Danube River cruise ships boast stylish lounges, panoramic observation decks, and inviting dining spaces that set the tone for a luxurious and comfortable journey.

5. Cabin Orientation: Settling into Your Home Away from Home

Upon boarding, head to your designated cabin to drop off your belongings and get acquainted with your home for the duration of the cruise. Cabins on Danube River cruise ships vary in size and amenities, but each is designed for comfort and convenience. Familiarize yourself with the cabin layout, storage spaces, and in-room facilities. Many modern cruise ship cabins feature large windows or balconies, providing stunning views of the passing landscapes.

6. Safety Drill: Ensuring Passenger Preparedness

Before the ship departs, passengers are required to participate in a mandatory safety drill. This important exercise ensures that everyone on board is familiar with emergency procedures and knows the location of life jackets and muster stations. Pay close attention to the safety briefing, as it provides valuable information that could be crucial in the unlikely event of an emergency.

7. Sail Away Celebration: Commencing Your Danube Adventure

As the ship sets sail, many cruise lines organize a sail away celebration on the upper deck. Passengers gather to witness the departure from the port, often accompanied by live music, refreshments, and a festive atmosphere. It's a perfect opportunity to mingle with fellow travelers, take photographs of the picturesque scenery, and soak in the excitement of the journey ahead.

8. Dining Options: Exploring Culinary Delights on Board

One of the highlights of a Danube River cruise is the culinary experience, and your first meal on board is eagerly anticipated. Most cruise ships offer a variety of dining options, from formal dining rooms to casual buffets and specialty restaurants. Familiarize yourself with the dining schedule and choose the option that suits your preferences. Some cruise lines also offer 24-hour room service, allowing you to dine in the comfort of your cabin.

9. Onboard Activities and Entertainment: Crafting Your Cruise Experience

Once you've settled in, explore the ship's schedule of onboard activities and entertainment. Danube River cruises often feature lectures, live performances, themed parties, and cultural enrichment programs. Whether you're interested in learning about the destinations you'll visit, attending a dance class, or enjoying a live music performance, there's a diverse range of activities to cater to various interests.

10. Meeting the Crew: Personalized Service Throughout Your Journey

The cruise ship's crew plays a pivotal role in ensuring a memorable and enjoyable experience for passengers. Take the time to introduce yourself to the crew members, including the cruise director, who can provide valuable insights into the upcoming itinerary and answer any questions you may have. The attentive and friendly nature of the crew contributes significantly to the overall ambiance of the cruise.

2.6. Getting Acquainted with Onboard Amenities and Services

Embarking on a Danube River cruise is not merely a journey through picturesque landscapes but a luxurious experience enhanced by a plethora of onboard amenities and services.

As you step onto the cruise ship, you're entering a floating haven of comfort and entertainment. In this section, we'll delve into the diverse offerings that make your time onboard not just enjoyable but truly unforgettable.

1. Luxurious Accommodations

Your home away from home, the accommodations on a Danube River cruise ship are designed to provide the utmost comfort and relaxation. From cozy cabins to spacious suites, each room is tastefully appointed with modern amenities. Expect to find plush bedding, panoramic views of the river, and well-designed interiors that create a serene retreat after a day of exploration.

2. Culinary Delights

One of the highlights of any cruise is the culinary experience, and a Danube River cruise is no exception. Onboard dining options range from elegant dining rooms serving gourmet meals to casual cafes offering a variety of cuisines. Indulge in a gastronomic journey as skilled chefs craft delectable dishes using locally sourced ingredients, bringing the flavors of the Danube's riverside destinations directly to your plate.

3. Relaxation and Recreation

Whether you're seeking relaxation or recreation, the cruise ship has you covered. Unwind in the spa with rejuvenating treatments, take a dip in the pool while enjoying panoramic views of the passing scenery, or hit the fitness center for a workout with a view. From yoga classes at sunrise to evening entertainment options, there's always something to suit your mood.

4. Enriching Entertainment

The journey along the Danube isn't just about the destinations; it's also about the entertainment onboard. From live music performances to cultural presentations, cruise ships host a variety of shows that celebrate the diverse heritage of the regions along the river. Enjoy themed parties, dance nights, and interactive events that create a vibrant atmosphere for passengers.

5. Educational Programs and Lectures

For those with a thirst for knowledge, Danube River cruises often offer educational programs and lectures. Enrich your understanding of the places you'll visit with talks from experts in history, culture, and geography. These sessions provide context to your journey, making each stop along the Danube more meaningful and insightful.

6. Concierge Services

Navigating through multiple destinations can be overwhelming, but cruise ships typically provide concierge services to make your journey seamless. From booking excursions to providing local tips, the concierge is your go-to resource for enhancing your onshore experiences. They can assist with everything from arranging private tours to recommending the best local eateries.

7. Onboard Shops and Boutiques

Indulge in a bit of retail therapy with the onboard shops and boutiques. Cruise ships often feature a selection of stores offering a range of products, from local crafts and souvenirs to high-end fashion and jewelry. It's an opportunity to find unique keepsakes that will remind you of your Danube River adventure.

8. Connectivity and Communication

While the allure of the Danube lies in its timeless beauty, staying connected is important. Most cruise ships offer internet services, allowing you to share your experiences in real-time with friends and family. Additionally, communication services like onboard phones ensure you're always connected in case of any need.

9. Child-Friendly Amenities

Families are welcome on Danube River cruises, and cruise ships cater to the needs of younger travelers. Kids' clubs, babysitting services, and age-appropriate activities ensure that children have a memorable and enjoyable experience. Parents can have peace of mind knowing that their little ones are entertained and well taken care of.

2.7. Recommended cruise line company

1. Viking River Cruises

Location: Offers Danube River cruises with departures from cities such as Budapest, Passau, and Vienna.

2. AmaWaterways

Location: Embark on Danube River cruises from various European cities, including Budapest, Vilshofen, and Nuremberg.

3. Uniworld Boutique River Cruise Collection

Location: Operates Danube River cruises departing from cities like Budapest, Passau, and Bucharest.

4. Crystal River Cruises

Location: Provides luxury Danube River cruises with departures from cities such as Vienna, Budapest, and Nuremberg.

5. Scenic Cruises

Location: Offers Danube River cruises departing from cities including Amsterdam, Nuremberg, and Budapest.

6. Avalon Waterways

Location: Operates Danube River cruises with departures from cities like Budapest, Vienna, and Passau.

7. Tauck River Cruises

Location: Embark on Danube River cruises from cities such as Prague, Budapest, and Vienna with this premium cruise line.

8. CroisiEurope

Location: Provides Danube River cruises departing from various European cities, including Budapest, Passau, and Vienna.

9. Emerald Waterways

Location: Offers Danube River cruises with departures from cities such as Budapest, Nuremberg, and Vienna.

10. American Cruise Lines

Location: Although primarily operating in North America, this cruise line occasionally offers Danube River cruises, typically departing from cities like Budapest and Vienna.

When planning a Danube River cruise, these recommended cruise lines provide diverse itineraries, exceptional amenities, and a range of experiences to suit different preferences. Whether you're seeking luxury, cultural enrichment, or family-friendly options, these cruise lines have established themselves as reputable choices for exploring the enchanting Danube.

CHAPTER THREE

DESTINATIONS ALONG THE DANUBE

3.1. Vienna: The Imperial City

Vienna, often hailed as the "Imperial City," invites travelers on a journey through centuries of opulence, architectural grandeur, and a vibrant cultural tapestry. Nestled along the graceful curves of the Danube, the Austrian capital beckons with a harmonious fusion of classical elegance and modern vibrancy. As you embark on a Danube River cruise, the approach to Vienna unveils a skyline adorned with majestic palaces, iconic landmarks, and the timeless strains of classical music drifting through the air.

Exploring the Imperial Legacy: A Stroll through Hofburg Palace

Vienna's imperial legacy unfolds like a captivating story, and the Hofburg Palace stands as a living testament to the grandeur of bygone eras. Once the winter residence of the Habsburgs, this sprawling palace complex invites you to immerse yourself in history. Begin your exploration by strolling through opulent rooms adorned with chandeliers and historic artifacts. Marvel at the Spanish Riding School, where the equestrian arts have been perfected for centuries, adding a touch of regal splendor to your visit. The Hofburg is not merely a collection of structures; it's a journey through the corridors of power and elegance that shaped the course of European history.

Musical Enchantment: Vienna's Harmonious Melodies

Vienna's association with classical music is legendary, and no visit to the city is complete without surrendering to its enchanting melodies. The Vienna State Opera, an iconic cultural institution, beckons you to experience the magic of a live performance. Whether it's the soaring arias of Puccini or the timeless compositions of Mozart, the opera house provides an immersive experience in the heart of Vienna's musical heritage. Alternatively, choose a traditional concert venue to revel in the sounds of Mozart and Beethoven. The streets themselves seem to resonate with the echoes of these maestros, creating a symphonic backdrop as you explore Vienna.

Culinary Delights: A Feast for the Palate

Vienna's culinary scene is a delightful journey into the heart of Austrian gastronomy. Begin your culinary adventure with a visit to one of the city's historic coffeehouses, where the atmosphere is as rich as the coffee itself. Indulge in a slice of Sachertorte, a decadent chocolate cake that has become a symbol of Viennese sweetness. For a more immersive experience, venture into Naschmarkt, Vienna's bustling market. Here, stalls overflow with fresh produce, artisanal cheeses, and aromatic spices. Don't miss the opportunity to savor Wiener Schnitzel, a crispy and flavorful delight that encapsulates the essence of Vienna's culinary prowess.

Practical Tips for Vienna-bound Travelers:

- Cultural Etiquette: Respectful behavior is appreciated when visiting historical sites and cultural venues.

Dress modestly when entering religious buildings and follow the rules of conduct.

- Transportation: Vienna boasts an efficient public transportation system, including buses, trams, and the U-Bahn (subway). Consider purchasing a Vienna Card for unlimited travel within the city.
- Language: While German is the official language, English is widely spoken in tourist areas. Learning a few basic German phrases can enhance your experience and interactions with locals.
- Currency: The official currency is the Euro (€). Ensure you have some cash for smaller establishments, but credit cards are widely accepted.

3.2. Budapest: The Pearl of the Danube

As your Danube River cruise gracefully glides into Budapest, the Hungarian capital unveils itself as the "Pearl of the Danube," an epithet well-deserved given its seamless blend of stunning architecture, thermal baths, and a vibrant cultural scene. Divided by the river into two distinct sides—Buda and Pest—Budapest offers a rich tapestry of experiences waiting to be explored by eager travelers.

Buda's Castle District: A UNESCO Gem

Embarking on your Budapest adventure, commence your exploration in the historic heart of Buda—the Castle District. Crowned as a UNESCO World Heritage site, this elevated expanse atop Castle Hill is a treasure trove of architectural wonders. The commanding Buda Castle stands as a testament to centuries of history, its impressive structure echoing tales of bygone eras.

Matthias Church, a jewel of Gothic architecture, beckons with its intricate details and awe-inspiring beauty. As you meander through cobblestone streets, the air is infused with a palpable historic ambiance, transporting you to a time when kings and queens strolled these very paths. Be sure to ascend to Fisherman's Bastion, where panoramic views of the Danube and Pest unfold, casting the city in a mesmerizing light.

Pest's Cultural Kaleidoscope: Crossing the Chain Bridge

The iconic Chain Bridge serves as your gateway to Pest, the bustling and culturally vibrant counterpart to Buda. Here, a kaleidoscope of experiences awaits, drawing you into the rich history and dynamic cultural scene of Budapest. The Hungarian Parliament Building, an architectural masterpiece along the riverbank, invites exploration. Marvel at its grandeur and learn about the political history that has unfolded within its walls.

Art enthusiasts will find solace in the Museum of Fine Arts, a repository of exquisite works spanning various periods and styles. Delve into the world of creativity and expression, appreciating the diversity of artistic endeavors housed within this cultural institution. A poignant pause at the Shoes on the Danube Bank memorial offers a moment of reflection, commemorating the lives lost during the Holocaust—a sobering reminder of Hungary's historical struggles.

Thermal Bliss: A Budapest Highlight

A visit to Budapest would be incomplete without indulging in its world-renowned thermal baths. Seek rejuvenation and relaxation at the Széchenyi or Gellért Baths, where thermal waters beckon weary travelers. The Széchenyi Baths, located in City Park, showcase an iconic neo-baroque architecture, providing a regal backdrop to your thermal experience. Immerse yourself in the healing waters, surrounded by grandeur, and let the soothing embrace of the baths be a tranquil interlude in the heart of this dynamic city.

3.3. Bratislava: Where History Meets Modernity

Bratislava, the capital of Slovakia, is a city that unfolds along the picturesque banks of the Danube, seamlessly blending its rich history with a modern and vibrant atmosphere. As your cruise ship docks at this captivating destination, you'll find yourself immersed in a cityscape adorned with medieval towers, baroque palaces, and contemporary structures, creating a unique tapestry that beautifully interweaves the old and the new.

Historical Stroll: Rediscovering Bratislava's Past

Embarking on a historical stroll through Bratislava's Old Town is like stepping back in time. This compact and walkable area is a treasure trove of architectural gems and cultural landmarks. St. Martin's Cathedral, with its soaring Gothic spire, dominates the skyline, showcasing the city's strong historical and religious ties. The cathedral, dating back to the 13th century, has witnessed centuries of change and stands as a symbol of Bratislava's enduring heritage.

The iconic Bratislava Castle is another must-visit landmark during your historical exploration. Perched on a hill overlooking the Danube, the castle offers panoramic views of the city and the river. Its impressive structure, blending various architectural styles, reflects the diverse historical influences that have shaped Bratislava over the centuries.

Wandering through the charming streets of the Old Town, lined with pastel-colored buildings, is an invitation to immerse yourself in the city's rich history. Hidden courtyards, cobblestone alleys, and a plethora of street art create an enchanting ambiance that beckons travelers to explore every nook and cranny.

UFO Observation Deck: A Panoramic Encounter with Bratislava

For a truly unique perspective of Bratislava, venture to the UFO Observation Deck perched atop the SNP Bridge. This futuristic structure not only adds a modern touch to the city's skyline but also provides breathtaking panoramic views of Bratislava and the winding Danube River.

As you ascend to the observation deck, the city unfolds beneath you, offering a bird's-eye view of historical landmarks, modern developments, and the flowing Danube. The juxtaposition of the futuristic design of the UFO Deck against the historical backdrop of Bratislava creates a visual feast for visitors, highlighting the city's ability to harmoniously blend the old and the new.

Local Flavors: Culinary Exploration in Bratislava

Bratislava's culinary scene is a delightful reflection of the city's diverse cultural influences. To truly savor the essence of Slovak cuisine, head to local markets like the Central

Market Hall. Here, you can explore stalls brimming with fresh produce, local delicacies, and traditional crafts.

A culinary highlight not to be missed is trying "bryndzové halušky," a quintessential Slovak dish. These potato dumplings, accompanied by a generous serving of sheep cheese and bacon, offer a tantalizing blend of flavors that exemplifies the heartiness and creativity of Slovak gastronomy. Engaging with local vendors and experiencing the vibrant market atmosphere adds a layer of authenticity to your culinary exploration.

3.4. Regensburg: A Bavarian Gem

Regensburg, nestled gracefully along the banks of the Danube, is a Bavarian gem that transports travelers to a bygone era with its medieval charm and architectural splendor. This UNESCO World Heritage site stands as a living testament to history, boasting well-preserved medieval structures, cobbled streets, and a skyline adorned with spires and towers. For those embarking on a Danube River cruise, Regensburg is a captivating stop offering a journey through time and a glimpse into the heart of Bavaria.

Historic Wonders: Unveiling the Essence of Regensburg

Regensburg's allure lies in its historic wonders, and a visit to the Regensburg Cathedral is a must for any traveler. This awe-inspiring Gothic masterpiece has stood for centuries, its intricate spires reaching towards the sky. As you step inside, the air is filled with a sense of reverence, and the play of light through stained glass adds to the ethereal ambiance. Wander through the Old Town, where every corner reveals a new architectural delight – from medieval merchant houses with charming facades to hidden courtyards steeped in history.

One of the iconic landmarks offering a picturesque view of the city and the Danube is the Stone Bridge. This medieval marvel, with its 16 arches and sturdy stone structure, has connected the Old Town with Stadtamhof for centuries. Strolling across this bridge not only provides a scenic vantage point but also a tangible link to Regensburg's rich past.

Thurn und Taxis Palace: A Glimpse into Royal Grandeur

Immerse yourself in the opulence of the Thurn und Taxis Palace, a highlight of Regensburg's architectural splendor. Originally a Benedictine monastery, the palace transformed into a royal residence that exudes grandeur. The sprawling complex invites exploration of its grand halls adorned with intricate decorations, manicured gardens that offer a tranquil escape, and the whimsical Hall of Fame. This hall, adorned with portraits of notable personalities, serves as a visual journey through the historical figures who have graced the palace's halls.

The Thurn und Taxis Palace not only offers a glimpse into the lives of royalty but also provides insight into the cultural and artistic heritage that thrived within its walls. It's a journey through time that complements the medieval tapestry of Regensburg.

Bavarian Gastronomy: A Feast for the Senses

Regensburg's culinary scene is a delightful celebration of Bavarian flavors, and a river cruise stop here presents a perfect opportunity to indulge in hearty, regional dishes. Head to a traditional beer garden, an integral part of Bavarian culture, to savor local brews under the shade of chestnut trees. The vibrant atmosphere, with communal tables and lively conversations, creates an authentic Bavarian experience.

Savor the rich taste of regional specialties, from the iconic Bavarian pretzels to hearty sausages and flavorful schnitzels. Don't miss the opportunity to pair your meal with a local beer, brewed with precision and tradition. The culinary journey in Regensburg is not just about the food; it's a cultural immersion that adds another layer to your exploration of this Bavarian gem along the Danube.

3.5. Belgrade: The Vibrant Serbian Capital

Belgrade, the dynamic Serbian capital, unfolds along the confluence of the Danube and Sava rivers, creating a mesmerizing panorama that sets the stage for a memorable stop on your Danube River cruise. As your cruise ship docks, you'll find yourself in a city that seamlessly blends history, modernity, and a lively cultural scene, offering a plethora of experiences for the eager traveler.

Kalemegdan Fortress: A Historical Panorama

Begin your exploration at Kalemegdan Fortress, a historic citadel perched at the confluence of the Danube and Sava rivers. This architectural marvel not only guards the city but also provides an unparalleled panoramic view of Belgrade. Wander through its sprawling park, where centuries of history unfold among ancient fortifications, statues, and verdant landscapes.

Exploring the Fortress: Kalemegdan is more than just a fortress; it's a living testament to Belgrade's multifaceted charm. Marvel at the well-preserved ramparts, where cannons from different eras still stand guard. The Military Museum within the fortress showcases Serbia's military history, featuring artifacts, weaponry, and exhibits that offer insight into the nation's past.

Scenic Beauty: The fortress park is a green oasis offering respite from urban hustle. Stroll along the paths, enjoy the shade of centuries-old trees, and soak in the breathtaking views of the rivers and the city below. It's a perfect spot for a leisurely afternoon, where history and scenic beauty converge.

Savamala District: Where Creativity Takes Center Stage

Dive into the contemporary side of Belgrade by exploring the Savamala district, an artistic neighborhood that pulsates with creativity and innovation. As you step into Savamala, you'll find yourself surrounded by vibrant street art, captivating murals, and a collection of eclectic cafes and galleries.

Street Art Wonderland: Savamala is a canvas where local and international artists have left their mark, turning the district into a dynamic outdoor art gallery. Every corner reveals a new masterpiece, from colorful murals that tell stories to thought-provoking graffiti that reflects the city's evolving identity. Take your time to explore the streets and alleyways adorned with this visual feast.

Creative Hub: Beyond the art, Savamala is a hub of creativity and cultural dynamism. The area hosts various events, from art exhibitions to music festivals, making it a lively center for artistic expression. Check the local calendar for any upcoming cultural events that might coincide with your visit, offering a chance to immerse yourself in Belgrade's contemporary scene.

Bohemian Quarter - Skadarlija: A Nostalgic Culinary Journey

Step into the past as you wander through Skadarlija, Belgrade's Bohemian Quarter, where cobblestone streets and traditional Serbian restaurants create a nostalgic ambiance reminiscent of bygone eras. This charming quarter is a culinary haven where history, music, and local flavors converge.

Ćevapi Delight: Indulge in local delicacies like Ćevapi, a traditional Serbian dish of grilled minced meat, often served with flatbread and condiments. The restaurants in Skadarlija offer an authentic culinary experience, allowing you to savor the rich flavors of Serbian cuisine while surrounded by live music and the bohemian spirit.

Live Music and Atmosphere: Skadarlija comes alive in the evenings with live music pouring out from the restaurants and cafes. The atmosphere is infectious, inviting you to linger, enjoy the music, and soak in the lively spirit of this cultural enclave. It's a perfect place to unwind, savor local delights, and immerse yourself in the vibrant energy of Belgrade.

3.6. Bucharest: Exploring the Lower Danube

Bucharest, the dynamic capital of Romania, serves as the grand finale of your Danube River cruise, offering a remarkable amalgamation of history, culture, and a flourishing modern identity. As you step off your cruise ship onto the bustling docks of Bucharest, the city unfolds like a vivid storybook, weaving its tale through architectural landmarks, lush parks, and a burgeoning arts scene.

Parliament Palace: A Monumental Marvel

Embark on your exploration by immersing yourself in the grandeur of the Palace of the Parliament, an architectural marvel that proudly claims the title of the world's heaviest building. This colossal structure is a testament to Romania's history and resilience. As you step inside, be prepared to be awe-struck by opulent interiors adorned with chandeliers, intricate marble detailing, and a sense of grandiosity that echoes the country's rich past. Guided tours provide insight into the building's history, construction, and its role as a symbol of Romanian strength and determination.

Old Town Charms: Unveiling Bucharest's Historic Soul

Wander into the heart of Bucharest through its Old Town, where narrow streets wind their way through a tapestry of historic charm. Discover hidden squares, each with its own story to tell, and stumble upon centuries-old churches that bear witness to the city's enduring history. The Stavropoleos Monastery, with its exquisite carvings and serene courtyard, stands as a living testament to the country's religious and artistic heritage. Meanwhile, the Lipscani district beckons with its vibrant energy, filled with cafes, boutiques, and lively shops, offering a glimpse into Bucharest's eclectic character and evolving identity.

Herastrau Park: Nature's Tranquil Embrace

For a moment of tranquility amidst the urban bustle, escape to Herastrau Park, a sprawling green oasis enveloping a serene lake. The park, a favorite among locals and visitors alike, offers various avenues for relaxation and recreation. Take a leisurely stroll along the tree-lined pathways, rent a boat for a peaceful cruise on the lake, or simply unwind in a lakeside cafe, soaking in the natural beauty that surrounds you. Herastrau Park provides the perfect setting to reflect on the diverse experiences of your Danube River journey, offering a peaceful contrast to the vibrant cityscape.

Practical Tips for Tourists: Navigating Bucharest

As you explore Bucharest, consider some practical tips to enhance your experience:

- Local Currency: Romania's currency is the Romanian Leu (RON). While credit cards are widely accepted, it's advisable to have some local currency for small purchases and markets.
- Language: Romanian is the official language, but English is commonly spoken in tourist areas. Learning

a few basic Romanian phrases can enhance your interactions with locals.

- Transportation: Bucharest has a well-developed public transportation system, including buses, trams, and the metro. Taxis are also readily available, but it's recommended to use reputable companies.
- Safety: Bucharest is generally safe for tourists. However, like any other city, it's essential to stay vigilant, especially in crowded areas, and keep an eye on your belongings.

CHAPTER FOUR

ONBOARD EXPERIENCE

4.1. Types of River Cruise Ships

River cruising has become an increasingly popular way for travelers to explore the world's waterways, offering a unique and intimate way to experience different regions. As the demand for river cruises has grown, so too has the variety of ships that cater to diverse preferences and travel styles. Understanding the different types of river cruise ships is crucial for selecting the one that best suits your needs. In this chapter, we will explore the various categories of river cruise ships, each offering a distinct experience on the water.

4.1.1. Classic River Cruise Ships:

Classic river cruise ships are characterized by their elegance, smaller size, and emphasis on providing a refined and personalized experience for travelers. Here, we delve into the details of what makes a classic river cruise ship a captivating choice for tourists seeking a timeless and comfortable adventure on the Danube.

1. Intimate Atmosphere:

Classic river cruise ships are designed to create an intimate and cozy ambiance. With a limited number of passengers on board, you can expect a sense of exclusivity that fosters camaraderie among fellow travelers. The smaller size allows for a more personalized experience, where the crew can cater to individual needs, fostering a warm and welcoming atmosphere throughout the journey.

2. Navigating the Danube's Waterways:

One of the key advantages of classic river cruise ships is their ability to navigate narrow and intricate waterways. The Danube River, with its diverse landscapes and charming villages, is best explored on vessels specifically crafted for its meandering course. Classic ships ensure a smooth and unhurried journey, allowing passengers to appreciate the breathtaking scenery as the ship gracefully glides through the heart of Europe.

3. Well-Appointed Cabins:

Classic river cruise ships prioritize comfortable and well-appointed cabins, providing a haven for relaxation after a day of exploration. Expect tastefully decorated rooms with panoramic windows, offering picturesque views of the passing landscapes. Many cabins come equipped with modern amenities, ensuring a comfortable retreat for passengers to unwind and rejuvenate during the cruise.

4. Fine Dining Experiences:

Culinary delights are an integral part of the classic river cruise experience. Onboard dining is a sophisticated affair, with gourmet meals prepared by skilled chefs. The emphasis is on regional cuisine, allowing passengers to savor the flavors of the Danube's diverse culinary offerings. Enjoy sumptuous meals in elegant dining rooms, often accompanied by panoramic views of the river.

5. Onboard Amenities:

While classic river cruise ships may be smaller in size compared to ocean liners, they are not lacking in amenities. Common features include cozy lounges, observation decks, and perhaps even a small fitness center. These ships are designed to provide comfort and leisure, ensuring that passengers have a variety of spaces to relax and enjoy the journey.

6. Cultural Exploration:

Classic river cruises on the Danube are not just about the ship; they are about the destinations along the way. Well-crafted itineraries include stops at historic cities, charming towns, and cultural landmarks. Shore excursions led by knowledgeable guides offer insights into the rich history and vibrant cultures of the regions visited, providing a well-rounded and immersive experience.

7. Socializing and Entertainment:

With a smaller group of passengers, classic river cruise ships encourage socializing and camaraderie. Enjoy evening entertainment, such as live music or cultural performances, in a more intimate setting. Social spaces on board, such as lounges and bars, become the perfect venues for sharing experiences with fellow travelers and making lasting connections.

4.1.2. Boutique River Cruise Ships:

These vessels redefine the concept of indulgence, offering a blend of intimate ambiance, personalized service, and top-tier amenities. For tourists considering a journey along the

Danube on a Boutique River Cruise Ship, here is a comprehensive guide to help you navigate this unique and opulent way of exploring one of Europe's most iconic waterways.

1. Intimate Atmosphere:

Boutique river cruise ships are characterized by their smaller size, fostering an intimate and cozy atmosphere. With a limited number of passengers on board, you can expect a more personal and exclusive experience. The smaller capacity allows for more attentive service and a chance to forge connections with fellow travelers in a relaxed setting.

2. High-End Accommodations:

One of the hallmarks of Boutique River Cruise Ships is the luxurious accommodations they provide. Suites are often more spacious and elegantly appointed, offering a haven of comfort and style. Expect premium amenities, plush bedding, and panoramic views of the passing landscapes. These ships prioritize comfort, ensuring that your onboard experience is as exceptional as the destinations you explore.

3. Gourmet Dining Experiences:

Culinary excellence is a cornerstone of Boutique River Cruises. Onboard dining options are curated to provide a gastronomic journey, featuring gourmet meals crafted with locally sourced ingredients. Enjoy a fusion of regional flavors and international cuisine, often accompanied by fine wines. The intimate dining spaces contribute to a refined and delightful culinary experience.

4. Exclusive Onboard Amenities:

Boutique river cruise ships often boast exclusive amenities that cater to discerning travelers. From spas and fitness centers to observation lounges and libraries, these vessels go beyond the standard offerings. Take advantage of wellness programs, attend enriching lectures, or simply relax in an elegant lounge while soaking in the picturesque views of the Danube.

5. Personalized Service:

The focus on a smaller passenger capacity allows the crew on Boutique River Cruise Ships to deliver personalized and attentive service. The staff is dedicated to ensuring your needs are met, creating a seamless and enjoyable journey. Whether it's a special request or assistance with planning excursions, the crew is there to enhance your overall experience.

6. Immersive Shore Excursions:

Boutique river cruises often include curated shore excursions that provide an in-depth exploration of the destinations along the Danube. Expert guides lead small groups, ensuring a more intimate and immersive experience. Whether it's a guided tour of historic landmarks, a visit to a local market, or a cultural performance, these excursions enhance your understanding and appreciation of the regions visited.

7. Themed Cruises and Special Events:

To add an extra layer of enrichment, some Boutique River Cruise Ships offer themed cruises centered around specific interests. Whether it's a culinary-themed cruise, an art and culture voyage, or a music-themed journey, these cruises allow passengers to indulge in their passions while cruising the Danube. Special events and onboard entertainment further enhance the overall experience.

8. Booking Considerations:

When considering a Boutique River Cruise on the Danube, it's advisable to book well in advance due to the limited capacity of these ships. Additionally, be sure to explore the specific itineraries offered by different cruise lines, as they may vary in terms of destinations, duration, and included excursions. Look for promotions or inclusive packages that align with your preferences.

4.1.3. Expedition River Cruise Ships:

Embarking on a Danube River expedition aboard an Expedition River Cruise Ship is an exhilarating adventure that promises a unique and immersive experience. These specialized vessels are designed for the intrepid traveler, eager to explore remote regions, encounter wildlife, and delve into the less-traveled corners along the majestic Danube. For tourists considering an expedition cruise on the Danube, here is a comprehensive guide with all the necessary information to make the most of this extraordinary journey.

1. Adventurous Itineraries:

Expedition River Cruise Ships on the Danube are carefully crafted to navigate through challenging waterways and reach destinations often inaccessible to larger vessels. These itineraries prioritize exploration, taking passengers to remote villages, nature reserves, and off-the-beaten-path attractions. Travelers can expect a blend of cultural encounters, wildlife sightings, and outdoor activities that go beyond the typical tourist experience.

2. Onboard Experience:

Expedition river cruise ships are designed to provide a comfortable yet casual atmosphere. While they may not boast the opulence of luxury cruise ships, they offer cozy accommodations suitable for the adventurous traveler. The focus is on creating a communal and laid-back environment, fostering camaraderie among passengers who share a passion for exploration.

3. Knowledgeable Expedition Leaders:

One of the highlights of an expedition cruise is the presence of experienced expedition leaders and naturalists onboard. These experts provide insightful commentary during excursions, enhancing the understanding of the local environment, wildlife, and culture. Passengers have the opportunity to engage in informative lectures, workshops, and discussions, gaining a deeper appreciation for the regions visited.

4. Exciting Shore Excursions:

Expedition cruises along the Danube prioritize shore excursions that align with the spirit of adventure. Activities may include guided hikes, wildlife safaris, kayaking, and visits to remote communities. Travelers can immerse themselves in the natural beauty of the Danube's landscapes and witness the cultural richness of lesser-known destinations.

5. Wildlife Encounters:

One of the defining features of expedition river cruises is the opportunity for wildlife encounters. The Danube River and its surrounding areas are home to diverse ecosystems, and passengers may have the chance to spot birds, mammals, and other fauna in their natural habitats. Expedition leaders guide wildlife-focused excursions, creating memorable moments for nature enthusiasts.

6. Casual Atmosphere and Flexibility:

Expedition cruises prioritize a relaxed and informal atmosphere. The dress code is typically casual, and the focus is on the adventure rather than formalities. Additionally, these cruises often provide flexibility in itineraries, allowing for spontaneous adjustments based on weather conditions, wildlife sightings, or unexpected cultural events.

7. Packing Essentials:

Travelers on an expedition cruise should pack accordingly for outdoor activities and varying weather conditions. Comfortable and sturdy walking shoes, weather-appropriate clothing, a hat, sunscreen, and binoculars are essential items. The cruise line will provide a detailed packing list, ensuring that passengers are well-prepared for the adventures ahead.

8. Responsible Tourism:

Expedition river cruises on the Danube prioritize responsible and sustainable tourism practices. Cruise operators often collaborate with local communities to ensure that tourism benefits the environment and local economies. Travelers are encouraged to follow Leave No Trace principles and respect the natural and cultural heritage of the regions they visit

4.1.4. Family-Friendly River Cruise Ships:

When it comes to embarking on a family adventure along the Danube River, opting for a Family-Friendly River Cruise Ship ensures that every member, from the youngest to the oldest, has a memorable and enjoyable experience. These specially designed vessels cater to the unique needs of families, providing a perfect balance of entertainment, education, and relaxation. Here's a comprehensive guide for tourists considering a family-friendly Danube River cruise.

1. Accommodations Tailored for Families:

Family-friendly river cruise ships prioritize spacious and comfortable accommodations suitable for families of all sizes. Many offer connecting staterooms or family suites to ensure everyone has their space while still staying connected. Additionally, amenities such as cribs and rollaway beds may be available upon request to accommodate the specific needs of younger children.

2. Kid-Friendly Activities and Entertainment:

One of the highlights of family-friendly river cruises is the array of kid-friendly activities and entertainment options available onboard. Dedicated youth clubs, game rooms, and age-appropriate activities are designed to keep children engaged and entertained. From arts and crafts to movie nights, these cruises provide a dynamic environment that ensures both parents and children have a fantastic time.

3. Educational Excursions for Young Minds:

To add an educational aspect to the journey, family-friendly river cruises often incorporate enriching shore excursions that cater to the interests of both children and adults. These excursions may include visits to historical sites, interactive museums, and hands-on experiences that make learning about the local culture and history enjoyable for the entire family.

4. Supervised Programs and Professional Staff:

Parents can also enjoy some well-deserved relaxation knowing that their children are in good hands. Family-friendly river cruise ships typically have trained and enthusiastic staff members who oversee supervised programs for children. These professionals are dedicated to ensuring a safe and enjoyable environment, allowing parents to partake in onboard activities or enjoy some quiet time.

5. Family Dining Experiences:

Dining on a family-friendly river cruise is a delightful experience, with options that cater to the diverse tastes of both young and mature palates. Flexible dining schedules, kid-friendly menus, and special dietary accommodations ensure that family meals are stress-free and enjoyable. Some ships may also offer casual dining venues, allowing families to have a more relaxed dining experience.

6. Onboard Amenities for All Ages:

Beyond the scheduled activities, family-friendly river cruise ships boast a range of onboard amenities suitable for all ages. From swimming pools to outdoor play areas, these ships are equipped to keep everyone entertained. Onboard movie nights, live performances, and themed parties contribute to the festive atmosphere, making the cruise experience a celebration for the entire family.

7. Practical Tips for Families:

- Pack essentials for children, including medications, favorite toys, and any comfort items they may need during the journey.
- Check with the cruise line regarding age-specific guidelines for kids' activities and childcare services.
- Plan shore excursions that cater to the interests and energy levels of the entire family.
- Communicate any dietary restrictions or special needs to the cruise staff in advance to ensure a seamless dining experience.

4.1.5. Luxury River Cruise Ships:

As a tourist considering a luxurious journey through the heart of Europe, understanding what makes a luxury river cruise ship special and the amenities it offers is essential for making the most of this indulgent adventure.

What Sets Luxury River Cruise Ships Apart:

1. Elegance and Sophistication:

Luxury river cruise ships are synonymous with elegance. From the moment you step on board, you'll be surrounded by refined decor, high-quality furnishings, and attention to detail. Expect a sophisticated ambiance that creates an intimate and exclusive atmosphere throughout your voyage.

2. Spacious and Lavish Accommodations:

One of the hallmarks of luxury river cruises is the spacious and lavishly appointed accommodations. Suites often feature panoramic windows, private balconies, and luxurious amenities. The focus is on providing a comfortable and indulgent retreat where passengers can unwind and enjoy the scenic beauty of the Danube.

3. Exceptional Service and Personalized Attention:

Luxury cruises pride themselves on delivering impeccable service. The onboard staff is dedicated to providing personalized attention to every guest, ensuring that your needs and preferences are not only met but exceeded. From attentive cabin stewards to skilled chefs, the entire crew is committed to making your journey memorable.

4. Gourmet Dining Experiences:

Culinary excellence is a cornerstone of luxury river cruises. Onboard dining options often include gourmet restaurants, showcasing world-class chefs who craft delectable dishes inspired by the regions along the Danube. Expect a diverse menu featuring locally sourced ingredients and a wine selection that complements the flavors of each destination.

5. Exclusive Shore Excursions:

Luxury river cruises go beyond the typical tourist experience by offering exclusive and immersive shore excursions. These curated outings may include private tours, VIP access to cultural attractions, and unique experiences that provide a deeper understanding of the destinations along the Danube.

6. Onboard Amenities and Entertainment:

Luxury river cruise ships feature a range of upscale amenities to enhance your journey. Enjoy wellness facilities such as spas and fitness centers, enriching lectures and workshops, and entertainment options that reflect the cultural richness of the regions visited. Whether it's a relaxing massage or a captivating performance, every moment on board is designed for your enjoyment.

What to Consider When Booking a Luxury River Cruise:

1. Itinerary and Destinations:

Review the cruise itinerary to ensure it aligns with your preferences. Luxury river cruises often explore iconic cities along the Danube, providing opportunities to delve into history, culture, and scenic landscapes.

2. Accommodation Options:

Explore the different suite categories available and choose one that suits your preferences. Some luxury river cruise ships offer expansive suites with additional amenities like butler service and private dining options.

3. Dining Preferences:

Consider the onboard dining options and whether they align with your culinary preferences. Luxury cruises often feature multiple restaurants, allowing you to savor a variety of cuisines during your journey.

4. Inclusive Amenities:

Check what amenities are included in the cruise package. Luxury river cruises often provide all-inclusive offerings, covering meals, excursions, gratuities, and even beverages, ensuring a hassle-free and indulgent experience.

5. Service Reputation:

Research the reputation of the cruise line and the specific ship you are considering. Reviews and testimonials from previous passengers can offer insights into the level of service and overall experience you can expect.

4.2 Cabin Options and Amenities

When embarking on a Danube River cruise, one of the key factors that significantly contributes to the overall experience is the choice of cabins and the amenities they offer. Your cabin becomes your home away from home during the journey, and the variety of options available ensures there's something to suit every traveler's preferences.

Choosing the Right Cabin for Your Danube Adventure

Danube River cruise ships typically offer a range of cabin categories, each designed to cater to different tastes and budgets. Understanding the options available can help you make an informed decision that aligns with your preferences and requirements.

1. Standard Cabins:

    - These cabins are often the most economical choice, providing a comfortable and cozy space for passengers.
    - Standard cabins are equipped with essential amenities such as a private bathroom, storage space, and a comfortable bed.
    - Ideal for travelers who plan to spend the majority of their time exploring onshore and see the cabin as a place primarily for rest and relaxation.

2. Balcony Cabins:

    - For those who value a private outdoor space, balcony cabins offer a personal balcony where passengers can enjoy scenic views and fresh air.
    - Balcony cabins often provide a more spacious layout, allowing for enhanced comfort during the cruise.
    - Perfect for individuals or couples who appreciate the serenity of the river and want to savor the passing landscapes from the privacy of their own balcony.

3. Suite Options:

    - Suites are the epitome of luxury on a Danube River cruise, providing ample space, premium amenities, and often exclusive privileges.

- Suite options may include separate living areas, larger bathrooms with upgraded features, and enhanced in-cabin services.
- Ideal for travelers seeking a premium and indulgent experience, suites offer a heightened level of comfort and personalized service.

Common Cabin Amenities

Beyond the different cabin categories, Danube River cruise cabins share a set of standard amenities designed to enhance the overall cruise experience.

1. Private Bathrooms:

- Regardless of the cabin category, private bathrooms are a standard feature. They are equipped with essentials such as a shower, toilet, and sink.
- Some higher-tier cabins may offer upgraded bathroom facilities, including larger showers, bathtubs, or premium toiletries.

2. Comfortable Bedding:

- A good night's sleep is crucial, and cruise cabins are equipped with comfortable beds to ensure passengers wake up refreshed and ready to explore.
- Passengers can typically choose between twin beds or a double bed, depending on their preference and cabin configuration.

3. Storage Space:

- Cabins are intelligently designed to provide ample storage space for luggage and personal belongings, helping passengers keep their living space organized.
- Depending on the cabin category, storage solutions may include wardrobes, drawers, and under-bed storage.

4. Entertainment Options:

- Cruise cabins are equipped with entertainment options, ranging from television and movie selections to music systems.
- While the allure of the Danube River and onshore excursions are primary attractions, these entertainment options provide a pleasant way to unwind in the cabin.

5. Climate Control:

- Cruise cabins are equipped with climate control features, allowing passengers to adjust the temperature according to their comfort.
- This ensures a pleasant environment, regardless of the weather conditions outside.

Cabin Upgrades and Extra Amenities

For those seeking an extra touch of luxury or additional perks, cruise lines often offer cabin upgrades and supplementary amenities.

1. Suite Privileges:

- Passengers opting for suites may enjoy exclusive privileges such as dedicated concierge service, priority embarkation and disembarkation, and access to private lounges.

2. Enhanced Views:

- Some cabins, especially those on higher decks, offer enhanced views of the river and its surroundings.
- Upgrading to a cabin with a better view can provide a more immersive experience, allowing passengers to take in the beauty of the Danube from the comfort of their cabin.

3. In-Cabin Dining:

- Suite options may include the convenience of in-cabin dining, allowing passengers to enjoy meals in the privacy of their cabin.

Choosing the Perfect Cabin for Your Danube Cruise

Ultimately, the choice of cabin depends on individual preferences, budget considerations, and the level of luxury desired. Whether you opt for a standard cabin for its simplicity, a balcony cabin for a touch of outdoor serenity, or a suite for a lavish experience, the key is to find the cabin that enhances your overall enjoyment of the Danube River cruise.

4.3. Dining Experiences on the Danube

The dining experiences along the Danube are a celebration of the rich and diverse culinary traditions found in the heart of Europe.

4.3.1 A Symphony of Flavors in Vienna

As you embark on a Danube River cruise, one of the culinary highlights awaits you in the heart of Austria – the imperial city of Vienna. Often referred to as the "City of Music," Vienna harmoniously blends its rich cultural heritage with a symphony of flavors that will enchant every food enthusiast on a river cruise adventure.

Viennese Culinary Tapestry:

Vienna's culinary scene is a tapestry woven with influences from Hungary, the Czech Republic, and Italy, creating a unique and delightful blend of flavors. The city's historic cafes and elegant restaurants offer a gastronomic experience that complements the grandeur of its architecture and the richness of its cultural history.

Must-Try Delicacies:

1. Sachertorte:

Start your culinary journey in Vienna with a slice of Sachertorte. This world-famous Austrian chocolate cake, with its layers of apricot jam and dark chocolate icing, is a delightful treat that has become a symbol of Viennese confectionery.

2. Wiener Schnitzel:

For a more savory experience, indulge in Wiener Schnitzel, a traditional Austrian dish featuring a breaded and fried veal cutlet. The golden and crispy exterior, coupled with the tender veal inside, is a culinary masterpiece.

3. Tafelspitz:

Another iconic dish is Tafelspitz, boiled beef served with horseradish and apple sauce. This dish, favored by the Habsburg monarchy, offers a taste of the imperial dining experience.

Viennese Coffee Culture:

Vienna's coffee culture is as famous as its pastries. Take the time to relax in one of the city's historic coffeehouses and savor a cup of Viennese coffee. The atmosphere is one of refined elegance, where conversations flow as smoothly as the coffee itself.

Wine and Dine:

Vienna is also renowned for its wine, particularly the Grüner Veltliner, a crisp and aromatic white wine that pairs perfectly with the local cuisine. Many restaurants offer an extensive selection of Austrian wines, allowing you to immerse yourself in the country's vinicultural traditions.

Dining Venues:

1. Historic Restaurants:

Vienna boasts historic restaurants that transport you to a bygone era. Places like Figlmüller, known for its massive Schnitzels, and Griechenbeisl, Vienna's oldest restaurant, offer not only delicious meals but also a glimpse into the city's cultural history.

2. Riverside Cafes:

For a more relaxed dining experience, explore the riverside cafes along the Danube. These charming establishments not only provide a picturesque setting but also offer an opportunity to enjoy local pastries and desserts while watching the river flow.

3. Culinary Events and Festivals:

Check the calendar for any culinary events or festivals taking place during your visit to Vienna. These events showcase the best of Viennese cuisine, with local chefs demonstrating their skills and presenting innovative takes on traditional dishes.

Practical Tips for Tourists:

1. Local Etiquette:

Familiarize yourself with local dining etiquette. In Vienna, it is customary to greet your fellow diners with a polite "Guten Appetit" before starting your meal.

2. Reservations:

Popular restaurants in Vienna can get busy, especially during peak tourist seasons. Consider making reservations in advance to secure your spot at the city's culinary hotspots.

3. Currency and Payments:

Ensure you have the local currency, Euro, for small purchases at cafes and markets. Credit cards are widely accepted in restaurants and larger establishments.

4. Tipping:

Tipping is customary in Vienna, and it is customary to leave a tip of around 5-10% of the bill. Check if a service charge has already been included in your bill before tipping.

4.3.2 Budapest's Culinary Kaleidoscope
Exploring Hungarian Cuisine:

1. Goulash – A Hearty Hungarian Staple:

Upon arriving in Budapest, immerse yourself in the country's rich culinary heritage by indulging in Hungary's national dish – Goulash. This hearty stew, traditionally made with tender meat, paprika, and a medley of vegetables, embodies the robust flavors of Hungarian cuisine. Whether sampled at a riverside cafe or in a cozy local eatery, Goulash provides a warm and authentic welcome to Budapest.

2. Langos – A Deep-Fried Delight:

For a delightful street food experience, venture into Budapest's markets and streets to discover Langos. This deep-fried flatbread, often served with various savory or sweet toppings, is a beloved snack among locals and tourists alike. The crispy exterior and soft interior make it a perfect treat to savor while exploring the city's vibrant neighborhoods.

Market Exploration:

Great Market Hall – A Culinary Haven:

No exploration of Budapest's culinary scene is complete without a visit to the Great Market Hall. Located at the heart of the city, this bustling market is a treasure trove of local produce, meats, and artisanal products. Stroll through its vibrant aisles, where the aroma of fresh spices and the colors of fruits and vegetables create a sensory symphony. It's an ideal spot to pick up authentic Hungarian ingredients or to sample local snacks and delicacies.

Wine and Dine:

Tokaji – Hungary's Liquid Gold:

Budapest's culinary journey is not limited to savory delights; it extends to the world of Hungarian wines. Don't miss the opportunity to savor Tokaji, Hungary's renowned sweet wine. This golden elixir, often referred to as "liquid gold," is produced in the Tokaj wine region and pairs wonderfully with the rich flavors of Hungarian cuisine. Many restaurants and wine bars in Budapest offer an extensive selection of local wines, providing a chance to explore Hungary's winemaking heritage.

Hidden Gems and Fine Dining:

1. Discovering Local Specialties:

Venture beyond the iconic dishes to discover hidden gems within Budapest's culinary landscape. Sample Halušky, traditional potato dumplings with sheep cheese and bacon, for a taste of authentic Slovak-Hungarian fusion. Explore cozy eateries tucked away in the city's historic quarters, where family recipes and regional specialties take center stage.

2. Fine Dining with a View:

For a more upscale experience, Budapest offers a range of fine dining establishments that seamlessly blend gastronomy with breathtaking views of the Danube and the cityscape. Indulge in a gastronomic journey that combines innovative Hungarian flavors with international influences, creating a culinary masterpiece that mirrors Budapest's cosmopolitan spirit.

Practical Tips for Tourists:

1. Local Etiquette:

While exploring Budapest's culinary scene, it's worth noting that Hungarian culture places emphasis on politeness and hospitality. It is customary to greet your hosts and express appreciation for the meal. Tipping is also common in restaurants, typically ranging from 10% to 15% of the bill.

2. Navigating Menus:

Menus in Budapest's restaurants often feature a diverse range of dishes. Don't hesitate to ask for recommendations or explanations of unfamiliar items. Many establishments have English-speaking staff, but a few Hungarian phrases for courtesy can enhance your dining experience.

3. Reservations and Peak Times:

Popular restaurants in Budapest, especially those with panoramic views, can get busy, especially during peak dining hours. Consider making reservations in advance to secure a table, especially if you have a particular restaurant in mind.

4.3.3 Bratislava's Quaint Eateries

For tourists embarking on a Danube River cruise, exploring Bratislava's quaint eateries is a must for an authentic and satisfying gastronomic experience.

1. Location and Atmosphere:

Bratislava's Old Town, with its cobbled streets and medieval charm, is the heart of the city's culinary offerings. Quaint eateries are scattered throughout this historic area, providing a perfect setting for visitors to immerse themselves in the local atmosphere while enjoying delicious Slovak cuisine.

2. Local Specialties:

The culinary landscape of Bratislava reflects a unique fusion of Slovak, Austrian, and Hungarian influences. Tourists can relish traditional Slovak dishes such as Halušky, potato dumplings served with sheep cheese and bacon, and Bryndzové Halušky, a variation featuring sheep cheese. These dishes embody the hearty and comforting flavors of Slovak cuisine.

3. Must-Try Dishes:

When dining in Bratislava, it's highly recommended to try the national dish, Bryndzové Halušky. This delectable dish combines soft potato dumplings with creamy sheep cheese and crispy bacon, creating a symphony of flavors. Another must-try is Segedínsky Guláš, a rich pork stew with sauerkraut and sour cream, offering a savory experience that captures the essence of Slovak comfort food.

4. Local Markets:

To fully appreciate Bratislava's culinary offerings, take a stroll through the local markets. The lively Main Square Market and the Old Market Hall showcase an array of fresh produce, regional delicacies, and handmade crafts. Here, tourists can engage with local vendors, sample fresh fruits, and perhaps pick up some authentic Slovak souvenirs.

5. Wine Tasting:

Slovakia boasts a burgeoning wine culture, and Bratislava is an excellent place to savor local wines. Many quaint eateries offer wine tasting experiences, allowing tourists to explore the diverse varieties produced in the surrounding vineyards. Don't miss the opportunity to taste Slovakian Riesling or the renowned Tokaj wine, both of which perfectly complement the local cuisine.

6. Recommended Eateries:

Bratislava's Old Town is adorned with a variety of quaint eateries, each with its own unique charm. Highly recommended establishments include "Modra Hviezda," known for its historical ambiance and traditional Slovak dishes, and "Slovak Pub," a lively spot offering an extensive menu of local favorites. These eateries not only provide delicious meals but also contribute to the overall cultural experience.

7. Culinary Events and Festivals:

Depending on the time of the visit, tourists may have the opportunity to participate in local culinary events and festivals. Bratislava hosts various food-related celebrations throughout the year, showcasing the city's vibrant gastronomic scene. From wine festivals to food markets, these events add an extra layer of excitement to the culinary exploration.

8. Cultural Etiquette:

When dining in Bratislava's quaint eateries, it's beneficial for tourists to familiarize themselves with local customs. Tipping is customary, typically ranging from 10% to 15% of the bill. Additionally, it's polite to greet the staff with a friendly "Dobrý deň" (Good day) upon entering establishments, enhancing the overall dining experience.

4.3.4 Culinary Exploration Beyond Major Cities

While the major cities along the Danube River, such as Vienna, Budapest, and Bratislava, boast renowned culinary scenes, the true essence of a Danube River cruise lies in the lesser-known gastronomic treasures waiting to be discovered beyond these urban centers. As a tourist on a Danube River cruise, you're in for a treat as you embark on a culinary exploration that goes beyond the bustling metropolises.

1. Melk: Wachauer Marillenknödel and More

As your river cruise meanders through the Wachau Valley in Austria, make a stop in the charming town of Melk. Here, culinary delights come in the form of Wachauer Marillenknödel – apricot dumplings that capture the essence of the region. These delightful treats are made with locally grown apricots, encased in a potato-based dough, and often served with a sprinkle of powdered sugar. Melk offers a delightful blend of simplicity and flavor, providing a unique taste of Austrian gastronomy.

2. Dürnstein: Apricot Indulgence

Dürnstein, another enchanting town in the Wachau Valley, is renowned for its apricot products. Take a stroll through the cobblestone streets and discover a variety of culinary delights featuring apricots. From artisanal jams and preserves to schnapps infused with the essence of this luscious fruit, Dürnstein offers a true celebration of apricot indulgence. Don't miss the opportunity to sample and perhaps purchase some of these delectable creations as souvenirs of your culinary journey.

3. Wachau Valley Vineyards: A Wine Lover's Paradise

The Wachau Valley is not only a haven for apricot enthusiasts but also a paradise for wine lovers. As your river cruise navigates through this picturesque region, you'll encounter terraced vineyards clinging to the hillsides. These vineyards produce some of Austria's finest wines, particularly Grüner Veltliner and Riesling. Take advantage of wine-tasting opportunities offered along the way, allowing you to appreciate the terroir of the region and the craftsmanship of local winemakers.

4. Culinary Experiences in Quaint Riverside Cafes

One of the unique aspects of a Danube River cruise is the chance to explore small towns and villages along the riverbanks. These places often harbor hidden gems in the form of quaint riverside cafes. These establishments, away from the bustling city centers, offer an authentic taste of local life and cuisine. Whether it's savoring a slice of homemade cake or enjoying a cup of freshly brewed coffee, these cafes provide a tranquil setting to immerse yourself in the culinary traditions of the Danube.

5. Local Markets: A Feast for the Senses

As your cruise makes stops in smaller towns, take the opportunity to explore local markets. These vibrant hubs showcase the best of regional produce, meats, and artisanal products. Engage with local vendors, sample unique delicacies, and perhaps pick up some edible souvenirs. It's a chance to connect with the heart of the community and appreciate the diverse flavors that define the culinary landscape along the Danube.

6. Embracing Authenticity in Local Eateries

Venturing beyond major cities allows you to embrace the authenticity of local eateries. In these establishments, you'll find dishes that reflect the cultural tapestry of the Danube's lesser-explored regions. From traditional potato dumplings to hearty stews, these local eateries provide a window into the culinary heritage of the places you visit. Engage with locals, ask for recommendations, and savor the flavors that make each stop along the Danube unique.

4.3.5 Onboard Culinary Delights

One of the highlights of this culinary journey is the exceptional onboard dining experience, where passengers are treated to a delightful array of flavors that mirror the richness of the Danube's cultural tapestry.

The Culinary Canvas Onboard:

Cruise ships sailing along the Danube are renowned for transforming mealtimes into memorable events. Onboard culinary experiences are carefully curated to showcase the best of regional specialties, ensuring that passengers get a taste of the diverse cuisines along the river.

From elegantly plated dishes that pay homage to local traditions to international cuisine that caters to various tastes, the onboard culinary scene is a culinary canvas that reflects the cultural diversity of the Danube's riverside destinations.

Themed Dinners:

One of the highlights of the onboard culinary experience is the themed dinners that take passengers on a gastronomic journey through the Danube's rich history and culture. These special evenings often feature menus inspired by the regions visited, offering a curated selection of dishes that represent the culinary heritage of the area.

Whether it's a Hungarian-themed night with hearty Goulash and Dobos Torte or an Austrian-inspired dinner featuring

Wiener Schnitzel and Sachertorte, themed dinners add an extra layer of immersion to the cruise experience.

Cooking Classes and Culinary Demonstrations:

For those who want to take their culinary experience to the next level, many Danube River cruise ships offer cooking classes and demonstrations led by expert chefs. Passengers can participate in hands-on sessions to learn the secrets behind preparing regional delicacies.

Imagine crafting your own traditional Strudel or perfecting the art of making Hungarian Chimney Cake. These interactive experiences not only provide a fun activity but also deepen the connection between passengers and the culinary traditions of the Danube.

Wine Tasting Along the Water:

The Danube region is renowned for its vineyards, and cruise ships take full advantage of this by offering onboard wine tastings. Passengers can savor the flavors of local wines, expertly paired with the cuisine served on the ship.

From the crisp and aromatic Grüner Veltliner of Austria to the sweet nectar of Hungary's Tokaji, these tastings offer a sensorial journey through the vineyards that line the Danube's picturesque banks.

Dining with a View:

One of the unique aspects of onboard dining is the ever-changing scenery. Whether you're enjoying breakfast on the sun deck as the ship glides through the Wachau Valley or savoring a gourmet dinner against the backdrop of

Budapest's illuminated skyline, every meal comes with a view.

The dining spaces on Danube River cruises are designed to maximize panoramic vistas, providing an unforgettable setting for passengers to enjoy their meals.

Catering to Dietary Preferences:

Danube River cruise lines understand the importance of catering to diverse dietary preferences. Whether you're a vegetarian, have specific food allergies, or follow a particular diet, the onboard culinary teams are well-equipped to accommodate various dietary needs.

Pre-cruise forms often allow passengers to communicate their dietary requirements, ensuring that every guest can fully enjoy the culinary journey without any concerns about their individual preferences.

4.4. Entertainment and Activities

Whether you're seeking cultural enrichment, outdoor adventures, or simply relaxation, the Danube offers a diverse range of experiences to suit every traveler's preferences.

4.4.1. Onboard Entertainment:

1. Cultural Performances:

Embarking on a Danube River cruise is not merely a passage through breathtaking landscapes; it's a transformative cultural immersion. Cruise lines curate an enchanting onboard experience by organizing cultural performances that bring to life the rich traditions of the regions you'll be traversing. As you sail along the Danube, immerse yourself in the vibrant tapestry of local arts and entertainment.

One of the highlights of these cultural performances is the opportunity to enjoy classical music recitals. The soothing melodies resonate through the ship, creating an atmosphere of elegance and refinement. Renowned musicians often grace the onboard stage, captivating audiences with renditions of timeless compositions. The notes of classical music seem to dance alongside the ship, echoing the cultural heritage of the Danube's shores.

In addition to classical music, traditional folk dances form an integral part of these cultural showcases. Talented dancers don authentic costumes, bringing to life the age-old dance forms that have been passed down through generations. The rhythmic beats and colorful choreography provide a glimpse into the folklore of the regions you pass, creating a dynamic and visually captivating experience.

To add an extra layer of authenticity, some cruise lines organize themed costume nights. These events invite passengers to don traditional attire, enhancing the immersive nature of the cruise. Whether it's the elegance of Viennese waltzes, the lively spirit of Hungarian folk dances, or the grace of Slovakian traditional clothing, themed costume nights allow travelers to step into the cultural shoes of the Danube's diverse heritage.

2. Educational Lectures:

As the ship gracefully glides along the Danube, a wealth of knowledge awaits through informative lectures delivered by experts. These educational sessions serve as windows into the Danube's past, providing valuable insights into its history, geography, and the cities that line its banks. Enrich your journey by delving deeper into the cultural and architectural wonders that await at each stop.

Expert speakers often share the significance of each port of call, unraveling the historical narratives that have shaped the Danube's diverse landscape. Discover the stories behind iconic landmarks, from the regal palaces of Vienna to the medieval charm of Bratislava. Gain a deeper appreciation for the architectural marvels that stand as testaments to the cultural legacy of the Danube region.

Geography comes alive through these lectures, allowing passengers to understand the natural beauty that surrounds the Danube. Learn about the diverse ecosystems along the riverbanks, from lush vineyards to scenic landscapes that change with each bend of the river. As you approach each city, the geography unfolds, offering a visual feast that complements the historical and cultural context provided by the expert speakers.

The educational experience extends beyond geography to encompass the cultural nuances that make the Danube a captivating destination. Dive into the traditions, customs, and contemporary life of the cities you'll visit, gaining a more profound understanding of the vibrant communities that call the Danube home.

3. Wine Tasting and Culinary Experiences:

A Danube River cruise is not just a visual and auditory feast; it's also a gastronomic delight. Indulge your taste buds in the flavors of the Danube through onboard wine tastings and culinary experiences that celebrate the region's diverse culinary heritage.

Wine enthusiasts will find the onboard wine tastings to be a highlight of their cruise experience. Local wines, each with a story to tell, take center stage as knowledgeable sommeliers guide passengers through tastings. From the crisp whites of the Wachau Valley to the robust reds of Hungary, the wines mirror the diversity of the landscapes you traverse.

Culinary demonstrations by renowned chefs further elevate the onboard experience. These skilled culinary artists showcase the artistry of Danube cuisine, providing passengers with an intimate look into the preparation of local dishes. From the aromatic spices of Hungarian goulash to the delicate pastries of Vienna, these demonstrations offer a sensory journey through the region's gastronomic delights.

Participating in these culinary experiences is more than a meal; it's a way to connect with the culture and traditions of the places you're exploring. The flavors of the Danube become a thread that weaves through your entire cruise, creating a delicious narrative that complements the historical and cultural tapestry of the region.

4. Themed Nights and Parties:

Cruise ships on the Danube often transform into floating celebrations, hosting themed nights and parties that infuse the journey with a sense of festivity. These events go beyond the typical cruise experience, creating a unique ambiance that allows passengers to socialize, dance, and revel in the joyous atmosphere.

One such highlight is the glamorous gala night, where passengers have the opportunity to dress up in their finest attire. The ship becomes a glittering venue, and guests can enjoy an evening of sophistication and elegance. The gala night is a perfect occasion to mingle with fellow travelers, creating lasting memories in a setting reminiscent of a bygone era.

For those seeking a taste of Bavarian culture, some cruises feature a Bavarian beer festival. Imagine the lively sounds of traditional oompah bands, the clinking of beer steins, and the aroma of hearty German fare. It's a lively celebration that brings the spirit of Oktoberfest to the Danube, complete with themed decorations and a jovial atmosphere.

Another memorable experience is the masquerade ball, where passengers can don masks and costumes for a night of mystery and intrigue. The ship's venues are transformed into magical settings, and guests can dance the night away in an enchanting atmosphere. The masquerade ball adds an element of playfulness to the cruise, fostering a sense of camaraderie among passengers.

In addition to these themed events, cruise ships often organize other parties and gatherings throughout the journey. Whether it's a sunset cocktail party on the deck or a themed dance night featuring music from the regions you're visiting, these festivities enhance the social aspect of the cruise, creating a sense of community among passengers.

4.4.2. Shore Excursions and Outdoor Adventures:
Guided City Tours:

Embarking on a Danube River cruise not only promises scenic vistas but also invites you to delve into the historical treasures of cities lining the riverbanks through guided city tours. These immersive excursions, led by knowledgeable local guides, offer a deeper understanding of each destination's iconic landmarks, architectural wonders, and the compelling stories that have shaped its identity.

In cities like Vienna, the guided city tour unfolds the grandeur of imperial palaces, such as Schönbrunn and Hofburg, as well as the cultural richness found in the Belvedere Palace. The guide unveils the historical significance behind each architectural marvel, providing context to the opulent past that shaped Vienna into the cultural capital it is today. Meanwhile, in Regensburg, the medieval charm comes to life as you explore its well-preserved old town, a UNESCO World Heritage Site. The guided tour unveils the secrets of the iconic Stone Bridge and the majestic Regensburg Cathedral, transporting you to a bygone era.

These guided city tours are not mere strolls through historic streets; they are curated experiences that ensure you grasp the essence of each destination. Guides share anecdotes, historical insights, and local perspectives, creating a narrative that connects you intimately with the cities along the Danube.

Cycling Excursions:

For those seeking adventure, many Danube River cruise itineraries offer cycling excursions along the scenic riverbanks. This allows you to embrace the natural beauty of the region at your own pace, pedaling through picturesque landscapes, charming villages, and sprawling vineyards.

Imagine cycling through the Wachau Valley, where terraced vineyards meet the meandering river. The cycling excursion offers a unique perspective, allowing you to explore hidden gems and experience the charm of riverside life. Cruise itineraries often provide well-maintained bicycles, ensuring a comfortable and enjoyable ride for both novice cyclists and enthusiasts alike.

Hiking and Nature Walks:

Nature enthusiasts can further connect with the Danube's pristine beauty through guided hikes and nature walks during port stops. These excursions take you off the beaten path, leading to hidden gems where you can witness breathtaking views, discover the local flora and fauna, and appreciate the tranquility of the Danube's riverside.

Whether it's a hike through the lush landscapes surrounding Dürnstein or a nature walk near the Devin Castle, each excursion offers a chance to escape into nature. Knowledgeable guides share insights into the ecological significance of the area, enhancing your appreciation for the natural wonders that flourish along the Danube.

Adventures for Thrill-Seekers:

For the adrenaline junkies, select cruise lines cater to thrill-seekers with optional excursions that go beyond the traditional. Imagine kayaking along the Danube, navigating through scenic stretches with an experienced guide providing commentary on the surrounding landscapes. Alternatively, soar above the river on a zip-lining adventure, gaining a bird's-eye view of the Danube's winding path.

For those seeking an even more elevated experience, some cruise itineraries offer hot air balloon rides. Drift above the river, witnessing the landscape unfold beneath you in a breathtaking panorama. These optional excursions provide a unique and thrilling perspective of the Danube and its surroundings, ensuring that the adventure-seekers among the passengers have ample opportunities to satisfy their craving for excitement.

Relaxation and Leisure:

1. Onboard Spa and Wellness:

While the Danube River cruise promises exploration and adventure, it also caters to relaxation and rejuvenation through onboard spa facilities. Many cruise ships feature wellness centers where passengers can unwind with massages, beauty treatments, and fitness classes. Whether you opt for a deep tissue massage to soothe tired muscles or a rejuvenating facial to invigorate the senses, the onboard spa is a sanctuary of tranquility.

Indulge in the serenity of a sauna or take a refreshing dip in the pool, all while enjoying the ever-changing scenery outside your window. The onboard spa and wellness facilities are designed to enhance your overall cruise experience, providing a perfect balance between exploration and self-care.

2. Leisurely Afternoons on Deck:

Embrace the unhurried pace of river cruising by dedicating tranquil afternoons to lounging on the deck. Comfortable chairs, refreshing drinks, and the soothing sounds of the Danube create the perfect setting for relaxation. As the ship gracefully glides along the river, take in the panoramic views of vineyards, historic castles, and charming villages that unfold before your eyes.

Whether you choose to immerse yourself in a good book, engage in leisurely conversations with fellow passengers, or simply close your eyes and let the gentle breeze whisk away your cares, the leisurely afternoons on deck become an integral part of the river cruise experience. It's an opportunity to unwind, reflect, and appreciate the beauty that surrounds you.

CHAPTER FIVE

EXPLORING CULTURE AND HISTORY

5.1 UNESCO World Heritage Sites Along the Danube

The Danube River, with its meandering course through Europe, is adorned with a tapestry of cultural, historical, and natural wonders. Among the jewels that embellish its banks, several sites have earned the prestigious title of UNESCO World Heritage Sites. These landmarks stand as testaments to the rich history and diverse heritage that line the course of this majestic river.

5.1.1 Vienna: Historic Centre of the Austrian Capital

Nestled along the banks of the Danube, Vienna, the imperial capital of Austria, is a city that encapsulates centuries of history, culture, and architectural brilliance. Recognized as a UNESCO World Heritage Site, the Historic Centre of Vienna is a testament to the city's significance in shaping European heritage. This designation, bestowed in 2001, encompasses a meticulously preserved area that seamlessly weaves together architectural masterpieces, cultural landmarks, and a rich tapestry of historical narratives.

Architectural Marvels:

At the heart of Vienna's UNESCO-listed Historic Centre stands St. Stephen's Cathedral, a Gothic masterpiece that has been a symbol of the city for centuries. Its intricate spire dominates the skyline, and the cathedral's interior boasts stunning stained glass windows, intricately carved altars, and the ornate catacombs. The Hofburg Imperial Palace, another jewel within the Historic Centre, served as the residence of the Habsburgs for over six centuries. The palace complex includes the Imperial Apartments, the Sisi Museum, and the Imperial Chapel, offering visitors a glimpse into the opulent lifestyle of the imperial family.

Belvedere Palace:

Adding to the architectural splendor of the UNESCO site is the Belvedere Palace. Comprising the Upper and Lower Belvedere, this Baroque masterpiece was constructed as a summer residence for Prince Eugene of Savoy. The Upper Belvedere houses a remarkable collection of Austrian art, including Gustav Klimt's renowned painting "The Kiss." The beautifully landscaped gardens connecting the two palaces provide a tranquil escape within the bustling city.

Historical Significance:

Beyond its architectural grandeur, Vienna's Historic Centre is a living testament to pivotal moments in European history. The Graben and Kohlmarkt, two of the city's main streets, bear witness to the medieval trade routes that once flourished in the heart of Vienna. The Spanish Riding School, situated within the Hofburg Palace, echoes the legacy of classical horsemanship that has been preserved for centuries. The significance of these sites extends beyond their physical presence; they are living artifacts that narrate the evolution of Vienna as a political, cultural, and economic powerhouse.

Cultural Vibrancy:

Vienna's UNESCO recognition is not only based on its architectural and historical importance but also on its vibrant cultural scene. The Vienna State Opera, located near the historic centre, is one of the world's premier opera houses, showcasing the city's commitment to the arts. The MuseumsQuartier, a cultural complex in the heart of Vienna, houses several museums and art institutions, contributing to the city's dynamic cultural landscape.

Preservation Efforts:

The designation as a UNESCO World Heritage Site underscores Vienna's commitment to preserving its rich heritage. Strict conservation measures ensure that the Historic Centre maintains its authenticity, allowing visitors to experience the city much as it appeared throughout history. The ongoing efforts to balance modernity with preservation showcase Vienna's dedication to sustaining its cultural legacy for future generations.

5.1.2 Budapest: Banks of the Danube, Buda Castle Quarter, and Andrássy Avenue

The UNESCO World Heritage Site encompassing the Banks of the Danube, Buda Castle Quarter, and Andrássy Avenue stands as a testament to Budapest's rich heritage and the unique confluence of Buda and Pest.

The Banks of the Danube:

The Banks of the Danube, a key component of Budapest's UNESCO recognition, offer a panoramic spectacle that epitomizes the city's grandeur. The riverbanks are adorned with iconic landmarks, creating a picturesque backdrop for the bustling life of the city. The view of the Hungarian Parliament Building, a neo-Gothic masterpiece, illuminated against the night sky, is a sight that lingers in the memory of every visitor. The Danube Promenade, stretching along the Pest side, provides an ideal vantage point for admiring the architectural marvels that line the river.

Buda Castle Quarter:

The Buda Castle Quarter, perched atop Castle Hill on the Buda side of the river, is a treasure trove of history and architectural splendor. The UNESCO recognition encompasses the historic complex, including the Buda Castle, Matthias Church, and Fisherman's Bastion. The Buda Castle, a symbol of Hungarian royalty, showcases a diverse range of architectural styles, from Gothic to Baroque. Matthias Church, with its vibrant roof tiles and stunning interior, stands as a testament to Hungary's religious and cultural heritage. The Fisherman's Bastion, a fairy-tale-like terrace with panoramic views, offers a captivating setting to appreciate Budapest's skyline.

Andrássy Avenue:

Andrássy Avenue, often referred to as Budapest's Champs-Élysées, is a grand boulevard that connects the city center with City Park. Lined with majestic buildings, elegant townhouses, and tree-lined promenades, Andrássy Avenue is a showcase of architectural finesse. The avenue is home to iconic landmarks such as the Hungarian State Opera House and the former aristocratic residences known as the "Palace District." The Millennium Underground Railway, the first metro line in continental Europe, runs beneath Andrássy Avenue, adding a historical layer to this stately thoroughfare.

Connecting the Two Halves:

The UNESCO World Heritage Site not only highlights the individual significance of the Banks of the Danube, Buda Castle Quarter, and Andrássy Avenue but also underscores the connection between Buda and Pest. The Chain Bridge, an iconic suspension bridge spanning the Danube, symbolizes the unification of the two sides of the city. The juxtaposition of the historic Buda Castle and the vibrant urban life on the Pest side creates a dynamic and harmonious cityscape.

Preservation and Cultural Significance:

The UNESCO recognition of Budapest's Banks of the Danube, Buda Castle Quarter, and Andrássy Avenue underscores the commitment to preserving the city's cultural and architectural heritage. The sites not only serve as popular tourist destinations but also as living monuments that reflect the evolution of Budapest over centuries. The ongoing efforts to maintain and protect these areas ensure that future generations can continue to marvel at the beauty and history embedded in Budapest's landscape.

5.1.3 Wachau Cultural Landscape
Nestled within the heart of Austria, the Wachau Cultural Landscape unfolds along the banks of the Danube, weaving a

captivating tale of natural beauty, historical richness, and viticultural prowess. Recognized as a UNESCO World Heritage Site, this stretch of the Danube River, spanning approximately 40 kilometers, is a testament to the harmonious coexistence of human activity and the environment.

Geography and Landscape:

The Wachau Valley is characterized by rolling hills, terraced vineyards, and picturesque villages that seem frozen in time. The riverbanks are punctuated by medieval castles, charming hamlets, and the iconic blue spire of the Dürnstein Church. The meandering course of the Danube through this cultural landscape creates a stunning panorama, drawing visitors into a world where the natural and cultural elements are seamlessly intertwined.

Historical Significance:

The history of the Wachau Cultural Landscape is deeply rooted in the medieval period. The Benedictine Abbey of Melk, perched majestically atop a hill overlooking the river, serves as a symbolic gateway to the Wachau. Dating back to the 11th century, the abbey has played a pivotal role in the region's religious and cultural development. Its Baroque architecture and opulent interiors reflect the wealth and influence of the church during the Habsburg dynasty.

Vineyards and Winemaking Tradition:

One of the defining features of the Wachau Cultural Landscape is its vineyard terraces, which have been cultivated for centuries. The region's winemaking tradition dates back to the Roman era, and today, the Wachau is celebrated for producing some of Austria's finest wines. The primary grape varieties cultivated in the area include Grüner Veltliner and Riesling. Visitors can explore the vineyards, taste the local wines, and gain insights into the winemaking process at the numerous wine estates dotting the landscape.

Charming Villages and Landmarks:

Dotted along the riverbanks are charming villages that seem to have stepped out of a storybook. Dürnstein, with its cobblestone streets and medieval architecture, is particularly noteworthy. The town's landmark is the Dürnstein Castle, where Richard the Lionheart was once imprisoned. The castle ruins stand as a silent witness to the region's historical significance.

Krems and Spitz:

The towns of Krems and Spitz further contribute to the cultural mosaic of the Wachau. Krems, a bustling town with a well-preserved historic center, offers a blend of contemporary life and historical charm. Spitz, on the other hand, is known for its vine-covered hills and the medieval fortress of Hinterhaus Castle. Both towns are gateways to the Wachau and provide ideal starting points for exploring the cultural and natural wonders of the region.

Conservation and Recognition:

The UNESCO designation of the Wachau Cultural Landscape as a World Heritage Site in 2000 underscores its global significance. The recognition extends beyond the physical attributes of the landscape to encompass the region's sustainable land use practices, preserving the delicate balance between agriculture, viticulture, and environmental conservation.

5.1.4 *Český Krumlov: Historic Centre and Castle*

Nestled in the picturesque landscape of the Czech Republic, Český Krumlov is a charming town that unfolds like a storybook, revealing a well-preserved historic center and a majestic castle, collectively recognized as a UNESCO World Heritage Site. This enchanting destination, situated in the South Bohemian Region, beckons visitors with its medieval allure and architectural splendor.

Historic Centre: A Medieval Tapestry

At the heart of Český Krumlov lies its historic center, a maze of cobblestone streets and squares that transport visitors to a bygone era. The town's layout, characterized by narrow alleys and charming squares, has remained remarkably unchanged since the Middle Ages. The colorful facades of the medieval houses lining the streets add to the town's vibrant atmosphere, creating a harmonious blend of Gothic, Renaissance, and Baroque architecture.

One of the central features of the historic center is the Svornosti Square, a bustling hub surrounded by historic buildings. Here, visitors can marvel at the intricate facades adorned with frescoes, explore quaint shops offering local crafts, and indulge in the welcoming atmosphere of local cafes. The charming town square encapsulates the essence of Český Krumlov's medieval charm.

Český Krumlov Castle: A Jewel on the Hill

Dominating the town's skyline is the iconic Český Krumlov Castle, perched on a hill overlooking the Vltava River. This architectural masterpiece is a testament to centuries of cultural and historical evolution. The castle complex, a fusion of Gothic, Renaissance, and Baroque elements, unfolds like a living history book.

The Castle's origins date back to the 13th century when the lords of Krumlov built a fortress to protect the important trade routes crossing the region. Over the centuries, it underwent expansions and renovations, with each era leaving its mark on the structure. The Cesky Krumlov Castle is not just a single building but a complex of palaces, courtyards, gardens, and towers, showcasing the evolution of architectural styles and tastes.

A highlight of the castle is the Baroque theater, one of the best-preserved theaters of its kind in the world. Visitors can step back in time as they explore the theater's intricately decorated interiors and marvel at the historical stage machinery. The castle's interiors also house a remarkable collection of art, tapestries, and period furniture, providing a glimpse into the lifestyle of the aristocracy through the ages.

Preservation and Cultural Significance

The inclusion of Český Krumlov's Historic Centre and Castle on the UNESCO World Heritage List in 1992 acknowledges the town's exceptional cultural and historical value. The preservation efforts undertaken by the local authorities and the residents have played a crucial role in maintaining the authenticity of the site. The commitment to safeguarding the architectural heritage ensures that future generations can continue to appreciate the medieval charm and grandeur of Český Krumlov.

Visitors to Český Krumlov not only witness the architectural marvels but also become part of a living, breathing cultural experience. The town hosts various cultural events and festivals throughout the year, adding a vibrant touch to its historic ambiance. The fusion of the past and the present in Český Krumlov creates a unique destination where history comes alive, and every corner tells a story.

5.1.5 Regensburg: Old Town with Stadtamhof

Regensburg, a medieval jewel nestled in Bavaria, Germany, boasts a UNESCO World Heritage Site that encompasses the Old Town along with the district of Stadtamhof, creating a harmonious blend of history, architecture, and cultural richness.

Historical Significance:

Regensburg's Old Town with Stadtamhof holds a significant place in European history. The Old Town, characterized by narrow cobblestone streets and well-preserved medieval architecture, reflects the city's role as a major trading hub during the Middle Ages. The Stone Bridge, a testament to medieval engineering, connects the Old Town to Stadtamhof, adding an extra layer of historical charm.

Architectural Marvels:

One of the highlights of the UNESCO-listed site is the Regensburg Cathedral, a masterpiece of Gothic architecture.

The cathedral, dedicated to St. Peter, features stunning stained glass windows, intricate sculptures, and a rich history that dates back to the 13th century. Visitors can climb to the top of the cathedral for panoramic views of the city and the Danube.

The Old Town is also home to numerous medieval towers, each with its own story. The iconic Tower of Peter provides an opportunity to climb its stairs and enjoy breathtaking views of the surroundings. The Old Town Hall, a fusion of Gothic and Renaissance styles, is another architectural gem that captivates visitors with its ornate facade and historical significance.

Stone Bridge and Stadtamhof:

The Stone Bridge, a medieval marvel that spans the Danube, connects the Old Town to Stadtamhof. Originally built in the 12th century, the bridge has been witness to centuries of history and is an integral part of Regensburg's UNESCO World Heritage Site. Crossing the bridge is like stepping back in time, with its medieval towers and panoramic vistas of the river.

Stadtamhof, located on the opposite bank of the Danube, complements the Old Town perfectly. This charming district features well-preserved medieval houses, quaint squares, and the historic Sausage Kitchen (Wurstkuchl), which has been serving traditional sausages for over 500 years. The combination of the Old Town and Stadtamhof provides a complete and immersive experience of Regensburg's historical and cultural richness.

Cultural Heritage:

Regensburg's UNESCO status is not only due to its physical structures but also the intangible cultural heritage that the city preserves. The Old Town with Stadtamhof is a living testament to the traditions, customs, and way of life that have evolved over the centuries. The annual Regensburg Dult, a traditional folk festival, adds a vibrant and celebratory atmosphere to the cultural tapestry of the city.

Visitor Experience:

Exploring Regensburg's UNESCO World Heritage Site is like stepping into a living history book. Visitors can wander through the narrow alleys, visit museums such as the Regensburg Museum of History, and enjoy the authentic atmosphere of traditional beer gardens. The city's commitment to preserving its heritage ensures that every corner tells a story, making it a must-visit destination for history enthusiasts and cultural explorers alike.

5.1.6 The Danube Delta

Nestled at the final stretch of the Danube River before it meets the Black Sea, the Danube Delta stands as a testament to the harmonious coexistence of water, land, and life. Recognized as a UNESCO World Heritage Site, this natural wonder is a sprawling labyrinth of waterways, marshes, and diverse ecosystems, offering a haven for an unparalleled array of flora and fauna.

Geography and Formation:

The Danube Delta spans over 5,000 square kilometers, making it the second-largest delta in Europe. Formed over millennia by the intricate interplay of river currents, sediment deposition, and the dynamic forces of the Black Sea, the delta is a dynamic and ever-changing landscape. It is a testament to the ceaseless dance between the river and the sea, resulting in a mosaic of habitats that support a remarkable variety of life.

Biodiversity:

The delta's significance lies in its extraordinary biodiversity. Home to over 300 species of birds, including pelicans, herons, and cormorants, it is a crucial stopover for migratory birds on their journeys between Europe and Africa. The reed beds, wetlands, and lakes provide a fertile environment for an abundance of fish species, contributing to the sustenance of the delta's rich avian population. Additionally, the delta is inhabited by a diverse range of mammals, amphibians, and insects, creating a thriving ecosystem that captivates scientists and nature enthusiasts alike.

Unique Flora:

The flora of the Danube Delta is equally impressive. The delta hosts a variety of plant species, with the expansive reed beds being a defining feature. These reed beds not only provide habitat and nesting grounds for birds but also contribute to the delta's natural beauty. Water lilies, willows, and other aquatic plants add to the colorful tapestry of the landscape, creating a visual spectacle that changes with the seasons.

Conservation Challenges:

Despite its UNESCO World Heritage status, the Danube Delta faces challenges that threaten its delicate balance. Human activities, including agriculture, fishing, and infrastructure development, can impact water quality and disrupt natural habitats. Climate change poses a further threat, with rising sea levels and altered precipitation patterns potentially impacting the delta's ecosystems. Conservation efforts are crucial to ensuring the continued health and vitality of this unique natural treasure.

Sustainable Tourism:

Recognizing the importance of responsible tourism, efforts have been made to promote sustainable practices within the delta. Eco-friendly tourism initiatives, guided birdwatching tours, and educational programs aim to raise awareness about the fragile nature of the ecosystem and the need for its protection. Balancing the allure of the delta with the imperative of conservation is a delicate task, and collaborative efforts are underway to strike this equilibrium.

Cultural Significance:

Beyond its ecological importance, the Danube Delta also holds cultural significance. The communities living in and around the delta have developed a symbiotic relationship with the natural environment. Traditional fishing practices, unique to the delta, have been passed down through generations, contributing to the cultural heritage of the region. The delta is not only a refuge for wildlife but also a living landscape shaped by human interactions.

5.2. Museums, Galleries, and Historical Landmarks

As you leisurely sail along the iconic waterway, here are some noteworthy stops that promise an immersive cultural experience.

Museums Along the Danube: Unveiling History's Treasures

1. Vienna, Austria: The Kunsthistorisches Museum

Situated along the Ringstrasse, the Kunsthistorisches Museum in Vienna is a cultural gem housing an extensive collection of fine art and artifacts. Visitors can marvel at works by European masters, including Vermeer, Rembrandt, and Velázquez. The museum's opulent interior is a testament to the Habsburgs' passion for collecting, providing a glimpse into the artistic legacy of the Austrian Empire.

2. Budapest, Hungary: Hungarian National Museum

For a deep dive into Hungary's history, the Hungarian National Museum in Budapest is a must-visit. From archaeological finds to medieval artifacts, the museum chronicles the nation's evolution, making it an enlightening stop for those seeking to understand the cultural tapestry of Hungary.

3. Bratislava, Slovakia: Slovak National Museum – Historical Museum

Perched atop Bratislava Castle, the Historical Museum of the Slovak National Museum showcases Slovakia's historical journey. The exhibits cover periods from prehistory to the

20th century, offering visitors insights into the country's rich past. The panoramic views from the castle also provide a stunning backdrop to the historical narratives.

Galleries: A Visual Feast along the Danube

1. Vienna, Austria: Belvedere Palace

The Belvedere Palace is not only an architectural masterpiece but also a gallery housing an impressive collection of Austrian art. Gustav Klimt's iconic painting, "The Kiss," is a highlight, capturing the essence of the Vienna Secession movement. Strolling through the palace's gardens adds an extra layer of visual delight to the artistic experience.

2. Budapest, Hungary: Hungarian National Gallery

Nestled in Buda Castle, the Hungarian National Gallery showcases Hungarian art spanning centuries. From Gothic altarpieces to 19th-century Romantic paintings, the gallery provides a comprehensive overview of Hungary's artistic heritage. The location itself, overlooking the Danube and Pest, adds to the enchantment.

3. Regensburg, Germany: St. Emmeram's Abbey

While not a conventional gallery, the art and architecture within St. Emmeram's Abbey in Regensburg are a visual spectacle. The opulent interiors and stunning frescoes transport visitors to a bygone era, offering a glimpse into the ecclesiastical artistry of medieval Germany.

Historical Landmarks: Icons Along the Danube

1. Passau, Germany: St. Stephen's Cathedral

The skyline of Passau is dominated by the majestic St. Stephen's Cathedral, a masterpiece of Italian Baroque architecture. Inside, the cathedral houses the largest cathedral organ in the world. Climbing to the top provides panoramic views of the city and the meeting point of the Danube, Inn, and Ilz rivers.

2. Melk, Austria: Melk Abbey

Perched on a hill overlooking the Danube, Melk Abbey is a Benedictine monastery that combines stunning architecture with a rich history. The abbey's library, adorned with frescoes, is a testament to the intellectual and artistic achievements of the Benedictine monks.

3. Cesky Krumlov, Czech Republic: Cesky Krumlov Castle

A UNESCO World Heritage Site, Cesky Krumlov Castle is a fairy-tale complex that transports visitors to medieval times. The castle's Baroque theater, charming courtyards, and panoramic views of the Vltava River make it a highlight of any Danube River cruise.

CHAPTER SIX

PRACTICAL TIPS FOR A SMOOTH CRUISE

6.1. Packing Essentials for Your Danube River Adventure

To ensure you make the most of your adventure, careful planning and strategic packing are essential. From versatile clothing options to practical accessories, here's a comprehensive guide on packing essentials for your Danube River cruise.

1. Clothing and Attire:

- Layered Clothing: The Danube's weather can be unpredictable, so pack layers to accommodate temperature variations. Lightweight sweaters, a waterproof jacket, and a mix of short and long-sleeved shirts are ideal.
- Comfortable Walking Shoes: Given the potential for exploring charming cities and historical sites, comfortable and durable walking shoes are a must. Choose footwear suitable for both cobblestone streets and light hiking trails.
- Formal Attire: Many cruises have formal or semi-formal evenings. Pack a dress or suit for such occasions to fully enjoy onboard dining and social events.

2. Travel Accessories:

- Travel Adapters: European power outlets differ from those in other regions, so bring suitable adapters to charge your electronic devices.
- Daypack or Tote Bag: A small backpack or tote is handy for daily excursions, allowing you to carry essentials like a water bottle, camera, sunscreen, and a map.
- Reusable Water Bottle: Stay hydrated while exploring by carrying a reusable water bottle. Some cruise lines provide refill stations on board.

3. Personal Care Items:

- Sunscreen and Sun Protection: Protect yourself from the sun's rays with a high SPF sunscreen, sunglasses, and a wide-brimmed hat.
- Toiletries Kit: While cruises often provide basic toiletries, having your preferred items can enhance your comfort. Include essentials like toothbrush, toothpaste, and personal hygiene products.
- Medications: Bring any necessary prescription medications and a basic first aid kit for unexpected situations.

4. Electronic Gadgets:

- Camera or Smartphone: Capture the breathtaking landscapes and historic landmarks along the Danube. Don't forget extra memory cards and charging cables.
- E-reader or Tablet: For downtime on the cruise, bring a device for reading or entertainment.

- Travel Power Strip: Given the limited outlets in cabins, a compact travel power strip can be invaluable for charging multiple devices simultaneously.

5. Documents and Essentials:

- Passport and Travel Insurance: Ensure your passport is valid for the entire trip, and consider travel insurance for added peace of mind.
- Cruise Itinerary and Documents: Print a copy of your cruise itinerary, boarding passes, and any reservations for onshore excursions.
- Credit Cards and Currency: Have both credit cards and local currency for purchases and tipping.

6. Miscellaneous Items:

- Collapsible Umbrella: Be prepared for sudden showers with a compact, travel-sized umbrella.
- Travel Sewing Kit: A small sewing kit can be a lifesaver for quick clothing repairs.
- Snorkeling Gear: If your cruise includes opportunities for water activities, pack snorkeling gear for a unique perspective on the Danube.

7. Entertainment and Leisure:

- Notebook and Pen: Document your journey and jot down memorable moments.
- Binoculars: Enhance your scenic views of the Danube and its surroundings.
- Playing Cards or Travel Games: Bring along compact games for leisurely evenings on the cruise.

By carefully considering these packing essentials, you'll be well-prepared for the diverse experiences that await you on your Danube River adventure. Tailor your packing list to your specific cruise itinerary, and don't forget to leave a bit of room for souvenirs from the enchanting destinations you'll explore along the way.

6.2. Health and Safety Considerations

In this comprehensive guide, we delve into the essential health and safety considerations for those embarking on a Danube River cruise.

1. Pre-Departure Health Preparations

Before setting sail on the Danube, it is crucial to prioritize your health in the pre-departure phase. This includes consulting with your healthcare provider to ensure that you are fit for travel. Discuss any pre-existing medical conditions, necessary vaccinations, and ensure that you have an ample supply of any required medications for the duration of the cruise. Additionally, obtaining travel insurance that covers medical emergencies is a wise step to take.

2. COVID-19 Protocols and Updates

In recent times, global travel has been significantly impacted by the COVID-19 pandemic. Therefore, staying informed about the latest travel advisories, entry requirements, and health protocols is imperative. Cruise lines operating on the Danube have implemented stringent measures to ensure the safety of passengers and crew. Familiarize yourself with the cruise line's COVID-19 policies, including testing requirements, vaccination mandates, and any quarantine procedures that may be in place.

3. Onboard Health and Safety Measures

Once aboard the cruise ship, passengers can expect a range of health and safety measures designed to create a secure environment. Enhanced cleaning protocols, hand sanitizing stations, and increased frequency of sanitation in public areas are common practices. Additionally, crew members are trained to respond promptly to any health concerns, ensuring a swift and effective resolution.

4. Medical Facilities and Services

Danube River cruise ships are equipped with onboard medical facilities and qualified medical staff to address any health-related issues that may arise during the journey. While major medical emergencies are rare, having access to medical assistance provides peace of mind. Passengers with specific medical needs should communicate these to the cruise line in advance to ensure appropriate accommodations.

5. Emergency Evacuation Plans

Though emergencies are unlikely, it is prudent to be aware of the cruise ship's emergency evacuation procedures. Familiarize yourself with the location of life jackets, emergency exits, and assembly points. Cruise ships conduct regular safety drills to ensure that passengers are well-prepared in the unlikely event of an emergency.

6. Dietary Considerations and Food Safety

For those with dietary restrictions or food allergies, communicating these requirements to the cruise line in advance is essential. Cruise ships on the Danube typically offer a variety of dining options, and the culinary staff is well-prepared to accommodate various dietary needs. Additionally, adhere to basic food safety practices, such as consuming only well-cooked food and avoiding street food during shore excursions.

7. Hydration and Sun Safety

Staying hydrated is crucial, especially when cruising under the European sun. Ensure you have access to an adequate supply of water, particularly during excursions. Apply sunscreen regularly, wear a hat, and use appropriate sun protection measures to prevent sunburn and heat-related issues.

8. Shore Excursion Safety Tips

While exploring the charming cities along the Danube during shore excursions, it's essential to stay vigilant. Be aware of your surroundings, follow the guidance of tour guides, and adhere to any safety instructions provided. Keep valuables secure, and use reliable transportation services recommended by the cruise line.

9. Responsible Alcohol Consumption

Cruise ships offer an array of beverages, including alcoholic options. It's important to consume alcohol responsibly and be aware of your limits. Excessive alcohol consumption can impair judgment and coordination, potentially leading to accidents or health issues.

10. Stay Informed and Be Proactive

Lastly, staying informed and being proactive about your health and safety is the key to a worry-free Danube River cruise. Attend safety briefings, read informational materials provided by the cruise line, and don't hesitate to ask questions if something is unclear. Being proactive ensures that you are well-prepared for any situation that may arise during your journey.

6.3. Currency and Payment Tips

The diverse countries along the Danube each have their own currencies, and understanding how to manage payments effectively can greatly enhance your overall experience. In this section, we delve into essential currency and payment tips tailored to the unique aspects of a Danube River cruise.

Understanding Local Currencies:

The Danube River traverses a multitude of countries, including Germany, Austria, Slovakia, Hungary, Croatia, Serbia, Bulgaria, Moldova, and Romania. Each of these nations has its own currency, and while some may use the Euro, others have their own monetary systems. Therefore, it's crucial to familiarize yourself with the currencies you'll encounter during your journey.

1. Euro Dominance:

In countries like Germany, Austria, and Slovakia, the Euro is the official currency. This simplifies transactions for travelers, as the same currency is used across multiple destinations.

2. Local Currencies:

Hungary (Forint), Croatia (Kuna), Serbia (Dinar), Bulgaria (Lev), and Romania (Leu) have their own distinct currencies. Familiarize yourself with the local banknotes and coins, and be aware of the exchange rates to avoid confusion during transactions.

3. Currency Exchange:

While major cities and tourist hubs may accept Euros, it's advisable to exchange some currency for each specific destination. Banks, currency exchange offices, and even some hotels offer exchange services. Keep in mind that exchange rates can vary, so compare rates before making transactions.

Payment Methods:

Understanding the local currencies is just the first step; choosing the right payment methods can significantly impact your convenience and security while cruising the Danube.

1. Credit and Debit Cards:

Credit and debit cards are widely accepted in most urban areas along the Danube. However, it's advisable to inform your bank about your travel plans to avoid any potential issues with card transactions in foreign countries.

2. ATMs:

ATMs are readily available in cities and towns along the Danube, providing a convenient way to withdraw local currency. Check with your bank regarding international withdrawal fees and currency conversion charges.

3. Local Currency for Small Purchases:

While cards are convenient, having a small amount of local currency in cash is advisable, especially for small purchases, street markets, or places that may not accept cards.

Navigating Dynamic Exchange Rates:

Exchange rates can fluctuate, and being mindful of these changes can help you make informed decisions during your Danube River cruise.

1. Real-Time Currency Apps:

Install currency conversion apps on your smartphone to stay updated on exchange rates. This will empower you to make on-the-spot decisions when exchanging money or making purchases.

2. Monitor Exchange Rate Trends:

Keep an eye on currency trends before your trip to anticipate potential changes. This can be particularly important if you plan to exchange a significant amount of money.

Safety and Security:

Ensuring the safety of your finances is crucial while traveling. Follow these guidelines to safeguard your money during your Danube River cruise.

1. Secure Payment Methods:

Opt for secure payment methods, and avoid carrying large sums of cash. Use hotel safes or other secure facilities to store valuables.

2. Contactless and Digital Payments:

Embrace contactless and digital payment options where available. They offer both convenience and added security, reducing the need for physical cash.

Local Tipping Etiquette:

Understanding the local tipping customs is an integral part of respectful travel. While tipping practices can vary across countries, a few general guidelines can be applied.

1. Research Tipping Norms:

Research tipping customs in each country you'll be visiting. In some places, service charges may be included, while in others, tipping is customary.

2. Carry Small Denominations:

Carry small bills for tipping, especially in local currencies. This ensures you can express gratitude for excellent service without complications.

6.4. Communication and Connectivity

Communication and connectivity play pivotal roles in ensuring that travelers can not only share their adventures in real-time but also stay informed and engaged throughout the journey. In this section, we'll delve into the various aspects of communication and connectivity that enhance your Danube River cruise.

1. Onboard Internet and Wi-Fi Services

One of the first considerations for many modern travelers is the availability of internet access during their cruise. Cruise lines operating on the Danube understand this need and, as a result, offer onboard internet and Wi-Fi services to keep passengers connected. While connectivity options vary among cruise operators, many provide Wi-Fi access in public areas and cabins.

Before embarking on your Danube River cruise, it's advisable to check with the cruise line regarding the internet packages they offer. Some cruises may include basic internet access in the overall package, while others may provide it as an add-on service. Understanding the internet options available will help you plan your online activities accordingly.

2. Communication Platforms and Social Media

Staying connected with friends and family is made easier than ever with the availability of communication platforms and social media. Most river cruise ships on the Danube are equipped with satellite communication systems that allow passengers to use messaging apps, make video calls, and share their experiences in real-time. Whether you're updating your social media accounts with breathtaking views of the Danube or sending messages to loved ones back home, these platforms ensure you're just a click away.

While enjoying the scenic beauty and cultural wonders along the Danube, consider utilizing popular communication apps such as WhatsApp, Skype, or FaceTime. These apps can help you bridge the distance and share the excitement of your journey with those who couldn't join you on the cruise.

3. Local SIM Cards and Roaming Options

For travelers who prefer to have a local number during their Danube River cruise, purchasing a local SIM card is a viable option. This allows you to have a local phone number and access data services without incurring hefty international roaming charges. Before purchasing a local SIM card, it's advisable to check the compatibility with your device and ensure that it covers the regions you'll be visiting.

Alternatively, some mobile carriers offer international roaming packages that can be activated for the duration of your cruise. While this can be a convenient option, be aware of the associated costs and ensure that the package covers the countries you'll be exploring along the Danube.

4. Wi-Fi Hotspots in Danube Cities

Exploring the cities along the Danube provides ample opportunities to connect to local Wi-Fi hotspots. Many cafes, restaurants, and public spaces in cities like Vienna, Budapest, and Bratislava offer free Wi-Fi to visitors. Taking advantage of these hotspots allows you to stay connected, update your travel plans, and even research the next exciting destination on your itinerary.

As you navigate through the charming streets and cultural landmarks of Danube cities, keep an eye out for Wi-Fi signs and ask locals for recommendations on the best spots to connect to the internet.

5. Communication Tips for Remote Areas

While the Danube River cruise takes you through vibrant cities and cultural hubs, there may be moments when the ship sails through more remote or scenic areas. During these times, communication signals may vary, and internet connectivity may be limited. It's advisable to plan ahead and download any essential maps, travel guides, or entertainment content before entering these remote stretches of the river.

Additionally, consider informing your loved ones about potential communication gaps during specific parts of the cruise, ensuring they are aware of the intermittent nature of connectivity in some areas.

6. Cruise Line Communication Services

Cruise lines operating on the Danube often provide dedicated communication services for passengers. This can include daily newsletters, information sessions, and even dedicated communication channels on the ship's entertainment system. Staying informed about onboard activities, port information, and any changes to the itinerary can enhance your overall cruise experience.

Before setting sail, familiarize yourself with the communication services offered by your cruise line. This proactive approach ensures that you're well-informed throughout the journey, allowing you to make the most of the cultural, historical, and scenic wonders along the Danube.

CHAPTER SEVEN

BEYOND THE CRUISE: EXTENDING YOUR DANUBE EXPERIENCE

7.1 Pre- and Post-Cruise Extensions

The allure of a Danube River cruise extends beyond the days spent on the ship, beckoning travelers to explore the enchanting destinations before embarking on the voyage and after disembarking. Pre- and post-cruise extensions offer an opportunity to delve deeper into the rich tapestry of Europe, adding layers to the cruise experience and creating a more immersive journey.

7.1.1: Pre-Cruise Exploration

Before setting sail on the Danube, savvy travelers often opt for pre-cruise extensions to maximize their time in the departure city and its surroundings. This not only helps mitigate the effects of jet lag but also allows for a more leisurely introduction to the region.

Vienna Unveiled: A Prelude to the Danube Adventure

Vienna, often the starting point of many Danube River cruises, is a city steeped in imperial history and artistic grandeur. Opting for a pre-cruise extension in Vienna opens a gateway to explore its iconic landmarks, including the Schönbrunn Palace, the Hofburg Imperial Palace, and the Vienna State Opera. Stroll through the historic streets of the

Innere Stadt, savoring the aroma of coffee wafting from traditional Viennese cafes. Engaging in a pre-cruise exploration in Vienna provides a more profound understanding of the city's cultural legacy, setting the stage for the river journey ahead.

7.1.2: Post-Cruise Unwind

As the Danube River cruise concludes, the adventure doesn't necessarily have to end. Post-cruise extensions offer a chance to linger in the final port of call or venture into nearby cities, enriching the overall travel experience.

Budapest Beyond the Banks: Extending the Danube Dream

Budapest, with its captivating blend of Buda and Pest, is a fitting conclusion to a Danube River cruise. Choosing a post-cruise extension in Budapest allows travelers to bask in the city's thermal baths, explore the historic Castle District, and meander through the lively Great Market Hall. Delve into the vibrant local culture by sampling traditional Hungarian cuisine at local eateries or attending a folk dance performance. A post-cruise extension in Budapest transforms the disembarkation point into an extended adventure, offering a seamless transition from the river cruise to the city's vibrant tapestry.

7.1.3: Crafting Your Own Extension

For those seeking a more personalized touch to their pre- or post-cruise experience, the option to craft a tailor-made extension provides flexibility and freedom. Consider exploring the picturesque Wachau Valley before the cruise or extending the journey to the captivating city of Prague after disembarking in Budapest.

Wachau Wonders: Crafting a Pre-Cruise Retreat

Nestled between Melk and Krems, the Wachau Valley presents an idyllic setting for a pre-cruise retreat. Explore charming villages like Dürnstein, where cobblestone streets and vine-covered hillsides create a storybook ambiance. Visit the Melk Abbey, perched atop a hill with panoramic views of the Danube. A pre-cruise extension in the Wachau Valley introduces travelers to the serene beauty of the Austrian countryside, setting the tone for the upcoming river voyage.

Prague Panorama: Extending Your Danube Adventure Beyond Budapest

For those seeking to extend their post-cruise experience, Prague offers a captivating blend of history and architecture. Wander through the Old Town Square, marvel at the astronomical clock, and cross the iconic Charles Bridge. Delve into the rich cultural heritage of the Czech Republic, exploring the Prague Castle and the historic neighborhoods that embody the city's medieval charm. A post-cruise extension in Prague transforms the journey into a multifaceted exploration, seamlessly blending the allure of the Danube with the timeless beauty of the Czech capital.

7.2 Alternative Travel Options Along the Danube

While river cruises are undoubtedly popular and provide a luxurious way to explore the Danube's beauty, there are alternative modes of transportation and unique experiences that cater to different preferences and interests. In this guide, we will delve into alternative travel options along the Danube, inviting adventurous travelers to consider a more diverse range of experiences.

1. Biking Adventures Along the Danube Cycle Path

For those seeking an active and immersive way to experience the Danube, embarking on a biking adventure along the Danube Cycle Path is an excellent choice. The well-maintained cycling route stretches for thousands of kilometers, following the river's course from Germany's Black Forest to the Danube Delta in Romania. Cyclists can choose segments that suit their fitness level and preferences, exploring charming towns, historic sites, and scenic landscapes along the way. This alternative allows travelers to set their own pace, stop at local cafes, and truly connect with the culture and natural beauty of the regions through which the Danube flows.

2. Riverboat Cruises for a More Intimate Experience

While traditional river cruises offer a luxurious experience, some travelers prefer a more intimate setting. Riverboat cruises provide just that – smaller vessels that navigate the Danube's waters, offering a more personalized and exclusive experience. These riverboats often have fewer passengers, allowing for a more intimate setting and the opportunity to forge deeper connections with fellow travelers. The smaller size of the boat also means it can access narrower channels and dock in smaller ports, providing a unique perspective on the Danube's hidden gems.

3. Train Journeys with Scenic Views

For travelers who enjoy the comfort and convenience of train travel, exploring the Danube by train offers a delightful alternative. Many cities along the Danube are well-connected by rail, allowing for a seamless journey through diverse landscapes. From the comfort of a train compartment, travelers can enjoy panoramic views of picturesque villages, vineyards, and historic landmarks. The train journey adds an element of nostalgia and romance, providing a unique perspective on the Danube's diverse regions.

4. Self-Drive Explorations for Flexibility

For the ultimate sense of freedom and flexibility, consider a self-drive adventure along the Danube. Renting a car allows travelers to explore off-the-beaten-path destinations, stop at viewpoints, and indulge in spontaneous discoveries. Driving along the Danube's scenic routes provides a sense of autonomy, allowing travelers to create their own itineraries and take detours to explore hidden treasures. This alternative is particularly appealing to those who relish the thrill of the open road and desire a more independent travel experience.

5. Cultural Immersion through Homestays and Local Experiences

Stepping away from the conventional modes of travel, immersing oneself in the local culture along the Danube can be a deeply enriching alternative. Consider opting for homestays in quaint villages, where you can interact with locals, partake in traditional activities, and savor authentic cuisine. This immersive approach allows travelers to gain a deeper understanding of the region's cultural heritage, fostering connections that go beyond the surface of tourist attractions.

6. Kayaking and Canoeing Adventures

For the more adventurous souls, exploring the Danube from the water's surface through kayaking or canoeing presents an exhilarating alternative. Paddling along the river allows travelers to engage with the natural beauty of the Danube at a more intimate level, navigating through gentle currents and discovering secluded spots inaccessible by larger vessels. This alternative is perfect for those seeking a more active and hands-on experience, with the added thrill of being one with the river.

7.3 Sustainable Travel Practices

Travel has always been a source of joy, enlightenment, and cultural exchange. However, as our awareness of environmental and social issues grows, so does the need for responsible and sustainable travel practices. In recent years, the concept of sustainable travel has gained prominence, urging travelers to consider the impact of their journeys on the environment, local communities, and cultural heritage. This shift in perspective is not just a trend but a necessary evolution in the way we explore the world.

Understanding Sustainable Travel

At its core, sustainable travel seeks to minimize the negative impacts of tourism while maximizing the benefits for local communities and the environment. This approach acknowledges the interconnectedness of our global community and the importance of preserving natural resources and cultural diversity for future generations.

1. Respect Local Cultures and Traditions

Sustainable travel begins with respect for the places we visit. It involves taking the time to understand and appreciate the local cultures and traditions. This includes learning about the customs, beliefs, and practices of the destination, and showing consideration for local norms. By fostering cultural respect, travelers contribute to the preservation of cultural heritage and the empowerment of local communities.

2. Support Local Economies

One of the most impactful ways to practice sustainable travel is by supporting local economies. Opt for locally-owned accommodations, dine in local restaurants, and purchase souvenirs from local artisans. This not only ensures that your money directly benefits the community but also helps in promoting economic sustainability. By choosing local services, you contribute to the prosperity of the destination and reduce the environmental footprint associated with mass tourism.

3. Minimize Environmental Impact

Reducing our environmental impact is crucial for sustainable travel. This involves making eco-conscious choices such as using public transportation, minimizing single-use plastics, and choosing accommodations with green initiatives. Additionally, engaging in activities that promote environmental conservation, such as wildlife sanctuaries and nature reserves, can contribute to the preservation of biodiversity and natural ecosystems.

4. Practice Responsible Wildlife Tourism

Wildlife tourism can be a powerful tool for conservation when done responsibly. However, it also poses a risk to the well-being of animals when not managed ethically. Choose wildlife experiences that prioritize the welfare of animals, promote conservation efforts, and adhere to ethical practices. Avoid activities that involve direct contact with wild animals, as this may contribute to their stress and disrupt natural behaviors.

Sustainable Travel in Action

5. Choose Sustainable Accommodations

The choice of accommodation plays a significant role in sustainable travel. Look for hotels, resorts, or guesthouses that have adopted eco-friendly practices. This may include energy-efficient systems, waste reduction programs, and water conservation initiatives. Many accommodations now hold certifications or memberships in sustainability programs, making it easier for travelers to make environmentally conscious choices.

6. Embrace Slow Travel

Slow travel is a mindset that encourages a deeper and more meaningful exploration of a destination. Rather than rushing from one attraction to another, take the time to immerse yourself in the local culture, connect with the community, and appreciate the natural beauty of the surroundings. By embracing slow travel, you not only reduce your carbon footprint but also gain a more authentic and enriching travel experience.

7. Offset Your Carbon Footprint

Air travel is a significant contributor to carbon emissions. While avoiding air travel entirely may not always be practical, there are ways to mitigate its environmental impact. Consider offsetting your carbon footprint by investing in carbon offset programs or projects. These initiatives support environmental projects, such as reforestation or renewable energy, to balance out the emissions generated by your travel.

8. Educate Yourself and Others

Knowledge is a powerful tool for change. Before embarking on your journey, take the time to educate yourself about the destination's history, environmental challenges, and cultural nuances. This knowledge not only enhances your travel experience but also empowers you to make informed decisions that align with sustainable practices. Share your knowledge with fellow travelers, encouraging a collective commitment to responsible tourism.

CONCLUSION

Reflecting on Your Danube River Cruise Experience

As the gentle waves of the Danube River fade into memory, it's time to reflect on the extraordinary journey that unfolded along its historic course. Your Danube River cruise experience was more than just a vacation; it was a captivating odyssey through the heart of Europe, offering a kaleidoscope of cultural richness, architectural marvels, and scenic wonders.

Embracing the Danube's Allure: A River of Stories

The journey began with the anticipation of exploring cities that have stood witness to centuries of history. From the grandeur of Vienna, where imperial palaces and classical music echo through the air, to the vibrant charm of Budapest, divided by the Danube and united by a shared history, each stop along the riverbank told a unique story.

Bratislava, with its cobblestone streets and medieval charm, offered a glimpse into a bygone era. The smaller, often overlooked towns dotted along the Danube revealed hidden gems and a more intimate connection with the local culture. The architectural wonders, from castles perched on hillsides to Gothic cathedrals that stood as testaments to time, left an indelible mark.

Cultural Immersion: Beyond the Surface

The cultural immersion was not confined to the grand monuments but extended to the heart of local life. Culinary delights danced on your palate, from savory goulash in Hungary to the delectable pastries of Austria. Engaging with locals provided a deeper understanding of their traditions and way of life, turning the journey into a personal exploration of culture.

Onboard activities and entertainment were not just diversions but enriched the overall experience. From lectures on the Danube's history to folk performances that brought local traditions to life, the cruise itself became a floating cultural enclave. As you reflect on your Danube River cruise, these moments of connection and understanding stand out as highlights.

Shore Excursions and Outdoor Adventures

The shore excursions were gateways to the essence of each destination. Exploring historic landmarks with knowledgeable guides added layers of context, making the experience more meaningful. Outdoor adventures, whether biking along the Danube's scenic paths or hiking to panoramic viewpoints, allowed for a deeper connection with the natural beauty that accompanied the journey.

Memorable Moments and New Connections

Reflecting on the journey, it's the small yet significant moments that linger. The camaraderie forged with fellow travelers during shared experiences, the breathtaking sunsets witnessed from the deck of the cruise ship, and the laughter exchanged over local delicacies—all these moments collectively create a tapestry of memories.

As you leaf through the photographs capturing these moments, the Danube River cruise becomes more than a travel experience; it becomes a part of your personal narrative. The memories of this journey will forever be etched in your heart, serving as a reminder of the vast tapestry of experiences that travel can weave.

Continued Exploration: Other River Cruises and Travel Adventures

While the Danube River cruise stands as a pinnacle of exploration, the world beckons with a multitude of rivers and destinations waiting to be discovered. Consider extending your river cruising adventures to other iconic waterways, each offering a unique blend of culture, history, and natural beauty.

1. Rhine River: Castles and Vineyards

Embark on a Rhine River cruise, meandering through Germany, France, and the Netherlands. This journey takes you past medieval castles perched on hillsides, picturesque vineyards producing world-renowned wines, and charming towns with cobblestone streets. Explore the iconic Lorelei Rock and immerse yourself in the romantic landscapes that inspired poets and artists.

2. Mekong River: A Taste of Southeast Asia

For a different cultural immersion, set sail on the Mekong River in Southeast Asia. Journey through Vietnam and Cambodia, witnessing the vibrant markets, ancient temples, and lush landscapes. The Mekong offers a glimpse into the rich traditions of the region, from floating markets to the intricate architecture of Angkor Wat.

3. Nile River: Unveiling Ancient Wonders

Step back in time on a Nile River cruise, where the ancient wonders of Egypt unfold before your eyes. Sail along the life-giving river, exploring iconic sites such as the Pyramids of Giza, Luxor Temple, and the Valley of the Kings. The Nile's banks are a living museum of history, offering a captivating blend of archaeological marvels and modern-day culture.

4. Amazon River: A Wilderness Expedition

For a truly adventurous experience, consider an expedition cruise along the Amazon River. Navigate through the heart of the world's largest rainforest, encountering diverse wildlife, indigenous communities, and the lush greenery of the jungle. Explore tributaries, embark on nature hikes, and embrace the unparalleled biodiversity that defines the Amazon basin.

5. Mississippi River: Southern Charm and History

Closer to home, the mighty Mississippi River invites you to explore the rich history and Southern charm of the United States. Cruise along the iconic river, stopping at cities like New Orleans, Memphis, and St. Louis. Immerse yourself in the music, cuisine, and cultural heritage that make the Mississippi a tapestry of American history.

6. Yangtze River: Majestic Landscapes of China

Embark on a Yangtze River cruise to witness the majestic landscapes of China. Cruise through the Three Gorges, marvel at the engineering feat of the Three Gorges Dam, and explore ancient temples along the riverbanks. The Yangtze offers a blend of tradition and modernity, providing a glimpse into China's diverse and dynamic culture.

Beyond Rivers: Diverse Travel Adventures

If your wanderlust extends beyond river cruises, the world offers an array of travel adventures waiting to be embraced:

Explore the Arctic: Set sail to the Arctic Circle, where polar landscapes, wildlife, and the Northern Lights create a mesmerizing tableau.

Safari in Africa: Embark on a safari adventure in the vast savannas of Africa, encountering the Big Five and experiencing the continent's diverse ecosystems.

Cultural Odyssey in Japan: Immerse yourself in the rich cultural tapestry of Japan, from the historic temples of Kyoto to the vibrant energy of Tokyo.

Trekking in the Himalayas: Challenge yourself with a trek in the Himalayas, where towering peaks, serene monasteries, and breathtaking vistas await.

Each travel adventure is a chapter waiting to be written, adding layers to your personal journey of exploration. Whether cruising along rivers or venturing into diverse landscapes, the world is a vast canvas inviting you to paint it with the colors of discovery. As you contemplate your next travel endeavor, let the memories of

past experiences fuel your curiosity and inspire new horizons. The beauty of travel lies in its ability to continuously unfold, offering new perspectives and enriching your understanding of the world.

Planning Your Next Adventure

As you consider your next travel adventure, take time to reflect on the aspects of previous journeys that brought you the most joy and fulfillment. Whether it's the cultural immersion, historical exploration, or the thrill of outdoor adventures, use these preferences as a compass to guide your future plans.

Research potential destinations and itineraries that align with your interests. Whether it's a river cruise along a different waterway, an expedition to a remote wilderness, or an exploration of vibrant cities, the world is brimming with possibilities. Engage with fellow travelers, seek recommendations, and gather insights to tailor your next adventure to your unique preferences.

Embracing Diversity in Travel

Diversity is the heartbeat of travel, and each destination holds a unique charm. Consider alternating between different types of travel experiences to create a diverse tapestry of memories. From the bustling markets of Marrakech to the serene fjords of Norway, every destination has its own story to tell and lessons to impart.

Embrace the opportunity to step out of your comfort zone. Venture into destinations that may not be immediately familiar but offer a chance to broaden your perspective. Whether it's navigating the intricate alleyways of a historic city or immersing yourself in the traditions of a remote village, these experiences contribute to personal growth and a deeper understanding of the world.

Connecting with Local Communities

One of the most enriching aspects of travel is the opportunity to connect with local communities. Whether it's sharing a meal with a family in a rural village or participating in traditional ceremonies, these authentic interactions create lasting memories and foster a genuine appreciation for cultural diversity.

Consider incorporating community-based tourism initiatives into your travel plans. Support local businesses, engage in sustainable practices, and contribute positively to the places you visit. By forging connections with the people you encounter, you not only gain insights into their way of life but also become a part of the global tapestry of human connection.

Adapting to the Rhythm of Exploration

Every travel adventure unfolds at its own pace, and embracing spontaneity can lead to unexpected joys. Allow room for serendipitous discoveries, whether it's stumbling upon a hidden gem in a bustling market or altering your itinerary to explore an intriguing detour.

Pack a sense of curiosity and openness as you embark on new adventures. Be willing to try local cuisines, partake in cultural festivities, and engage in activities that challenge preconceived notions. The beauty of travel lies in its ability to transcend the ordinary, offering moments of awe and inspiration that linger in your heart.

Preserving and Cherishing Memories

As you continue to explore the world, take the time to preserve and cherish the memories created along the way. Document your experiences through journals, photographs, and mementos that serve as tangible reminders of the places you've visited and the people you've met.

Share your travel stories with friends and family, creating a collective tapestry of experiences. Through storytelling, you not only relive your adventures but also inspire others to embark on their own journeys of discovery. Travel, in its essence, becomes a gift that keeps on giving, fostering a sense of interconnectedness and shared humanity.